DEDICATION

For Stan, my Dad and inspiration.

'LIFE'S A BALL'

'LIFE'S A BALL'

Ian Liversedge:
The Highs and Lows of a Football Physio

David Mitchell

authorHOUSE®

AuthorHouse™ UK Ltd.
1663 Liberty Drive
Bloomington, IN 47403 USA
www.authorhouse.co.uk
Phone: 0800.197.4150

Published by AuthorHouse 05/29/2014

ISBN: 978-1-4969-8077-9 (sc)
ISBN: 978-1-4969-8078-6 (hc)
ISBN: 978-1-4969-8079-3 (e)

CONTENTS

INTRODUCTION

The plan was to do this book with my Dad. Stan's exact words were, 'When you finish we'll do a book together. But when you do you won't get a job in football again.' He had all sorts of reasons for saying that. I knew that many of the things I got up to didn't impress him at all.

Stan would have loved to have seen it through after planting the seed in my mind. He was well-placed to help me having earned his living by writing about the game. He worked as northern Deputy Sports Editor of the 'People' newspaper and as Sports Editor at the 'Liverpool Echo' as well as writing a number of books about football in Merseyside and Manchester. Sadly, he passed away in 1997.

I'm known through the game by the nickname 'SOSS' so I'd better explain all before we start. It came about in the early days when I was a semi-pro and it's stuck ever since. There have been a few theories about its derivation but it comes from the name 'Liversedge' which then became 'liver sausage' then 'SOSS'. Easy!

My thanks go to Joe Royle for writing the foreword. Joe and I shared some wonderful times at Oldham Athletic in the 1980's and 1990's and if I could go back to any one of my clubs for just one day it would be Boundary Park during the time we put the club on the football map. Being in the inaugural season of the Premier League and two FA Cup semi-finals shouldn't happen to unfashionable clubs like Oldham but we lived the dream.

I met two of Joe Royle's sons in Smokies, a club in Ashton-under-Lyme near Manchester. I've known them since they were young. They came up and said to me,

'You know all these stories my Dad tells about you? Are they true?'

'Yes, every single one,' I replied. They couldn't stop laughing!

Aside from Joe, I have been fortunate to work for some great managers who have not only taught me much about football but provided me with wisdom and advice that has benefited me in my life. Bryan Hamilton is a wonderful guy who gave me first opportunity and later took me into the Irish job. Arthur Cox taught so much in such a little time. Stan Ternent was influential, Micky Mellon brought me back into the game and John Coleman taught me a lot about the value of money.

Then there's my good mate Ronnie Evans. I've been through thick and thin with Ronnie and he has never once judged me. The same applies to Neil Colbourne, my mate in Benidorm. I met Neil playing football in Wales in the 1970s and we've been great pals ever since. Neil used to take me in after marriage breakdowns. He was always there to sort me out and send me on my way again.

Finally, I met David Mitchell at Fleetwood Town some five years ago. I mentioned the possibility of a book one day after training and over the last year or so we have enjoyed regular chats over cups of coffee at the Tickled Trout near Preston where the book took shape. I am grateful to David for making sense of my thoughts and putting into the public domain a story that I never thought I would see after my Dad died.

ACKNOWLEDGEMENTS

Ian and David would like to thank the following for permission to use photographs:

The 'Oldham Evening Chronicle'

'Burnley Express'

Derick Thomas, Fleetwood Town Football Club's official photographer

Peter Hilton Photography, Macclesfield Town's official photographer.

Mark Wilson, Fleetwood Town photographer

Also,

Tony Bugby for allowing us to use an extract from his book 'Pinch Me Not', which celebrates the twentieth anniversary of Oldham Athletic's sensational 1989-90 season, and for granting an interview so that we could tap into his extensive knowledge of Oldham Athletic.

Dany Robson for valuable background information on Accrington Stanley's recent history.

Joe Royle for a session of brilliant anecdotes about 'SOSS' and times enjoyed at Oldham Athletic as well as agreeing to write the foreword.

Chris Lucketti for background information about days at Huddersfield Town.

Micky Mellon for reflections on life at Burnley and with Fleetwood Town.

Susan Mitchell, my wife, and patient proof reader.

Keith Clark and Howard Rose for help in reproducing photographs.

Front cover: Image by kind permission of Derick Thomas, Fleetwood Town Football Club.

Back cover: 'A Helping Hand', picture courtesy of Peter Hilton Photography

Cover design based on an original idea by Gillian Mitchell

FOREWORD

BY JOE ROYLE

Whenever I'm asked, 'Which player gave you most trouble at Oldham?' I'd reply, 'The physio!' I've even fished him out of jail at four in the morning! It was August 1992 and we were in London ahead of our first game in the Premier League, against Chelsea. It was to be a massive occasion for our football club.

We had the 'MASH' unit at Oldham. The name came from the popular film about the staff at an army hospital in the Korean War and we gave it to our physiotherapists, SOSS and Ronnie Evans. They liked a drink and I liked one with them but there always came a point where I left them to their own devices. I got a phone call about four in the morning from the hotel manager, 'Your physio's been taken to the local jail for attacking one of our bouncers.'

'What's he done?' I replied. 'Butted him in the kneecap or something?'

Well, what happened was that my little mate had tried to take his own bottle into the club at the hotel. The fella being officious had said something which offended SOSS who had risen up on his tiptoes and had a go back.

I've gone to SOSS's room to check out that the story is true. The door was open. Ronnie was in bed and I couldn't even wake him. I woke Rod Adams, one of the Oldham directors and also one of my best mates.

I took him down to the police station with me and met the warrant officer. I remember it as if it was yesterday.

'I've come to see about Mr. Liversedge.'

'You'd better get him out quickly. We're very close to charging him for causing an affray. He's facing a charge of wrecking the cell.'

How can you wreck a cell when there's nothing in it?! Anyway, the warrant officer took us into this room and all you could hear was SOSS effing and jeffing about who he was going to sue. He was obviously very drunk and very agitated.

They brought him out and he's still creating. I got him by the ear and said, 'Just shut up and let's get out of this place.'

Next day he was very sheepish and we got a great opening draw at Stamford Bridge. He'll probably deny everything about the night before when he mentions this story in the book but take it from me, he eventually did admit it was his fault.

SOSS has had his fair share of problems away from football and a few marriages along the way. He invited me to one of them and I couldn't go. I was desperately sorry to be away because I love the little fella so I just said,

'Sorry, I can't make it, mate, but I'll come to your next one!'

I went through his first divorce with him and told him straight,

'I'm not going through a second one with you.'

He met his second wife at the squash club when we played. He saw Jean and her friend on court and was smitten. He was head over heels in love with a beautiful and lovely lady. There followed a period where he'd come in late to work, unshaven and looking like a tramp's overcoat. He'd been up to the small hours the night before, out with Jean and drinking. He almost drank himself into oblivion at the time. He was also feeling the guilt trip over Joy, his first wife. Football became like a release for him. He'd come in, put on a pair of shorts and go out with the lads. He would be dishing and taking the banter.

I was working with my physio and dealing with him at the same time. However, because he was such a good professional, he was a cause worth fighting for.

I knew his dad, Stan, and did a couple of books with him about Everton. Stan was an old-school journalist who kept confidences and was as straight and as serious as his son was the opposite.

SOSS was a big part of our success at Oldham in the 80s and 90s. We giggled our way through ten years. I read one day about a manager who had lost his job and that he wouldn't let his players laugh or smile in training. Can you believe that? You get people who make others laugh and it makes the job far easier. Even through the bad times at Oldham, and there weren't many of them, we would always have a laugh. I look at the Premier League today and am convinced we would have survived comfortably. Players of the calibre of Rick Holden, Ian Marshall, Denis Irwin, Earl Barrett and Richard Jobson all went on to play for other top-flight clubs.

SOSS had a weekly calendar which went Monday, Tuesday, Wednesday, Thursday, Fuck off day! The point was that if you weren't fit on Friday you were no use. Come back another time.

We'll always be mates. Despite his exploits, the man's a top physio. I never had a complaint about SOSS's physiotherapy work. He was a dedicated professional through and through. Despite not having a big squad I always trusted him to make the right decision regarding injuries. There was no point in pressurising him. He had the medical experience after all. I always knew he was right. 'That's what I employ you for,' I would tell him.

His judgements were always spot on and he was straightforward and matter-of-fact. I remember Ian Olney going down at West Ham. SOSS came back to the bench and just said,

'This is bad. He's in a mess.'

It looked such an innocuous injury at the time but SOSS knew it was serious. The lad barely played again, just a few outings in non-league, which was a shame because his goals kept us up one season. Ian was one of those where the fans didn't appreciate how good he was and SOSS was, regrettably, spot on with his diagnosis.

He certainly knew his players. Certain ones would go down and I'd say to him,

'You'd better get on, mate.'

'He'll be alright,' the reply came back.

'Are you sure?'

'Yeah, he's fine.' And he would be.

This kind of judgement led to a call from Northern Ireland manager Bryan Hamilton who approached me for permission to take SOSS as physio. I told Bryan,

'He's got an exaggerated sense of mischief but he's a very good physio'.

International football followed and I'm sure he'll be telling you about it in his own words.

SOSS had a passion for annoying linesmen. In fact, he had a go at everyone, even me. I remember coming back on the coach after getting beat easily at Carlisle. He started throwing cans back over his head. One caught Andy Goram who came straight down and punched SOSS who ended up with three stitches in a head wound. I could cope with that but Andy broke his bloody hand and he was our goalkeeper! It was hard enough to keep that incident from the board otherwise he'd have been out of the club. There was often an angry man out there on the touchline but after the game it was back to normal. He used to be even worse on Friday nights in our 5-a-sides. I remember him once picking a fight with Willie Morgan against a wall in the gym.

Despite not being the best of time-keepers I always knew where SOSS was on a Saturday. I valued him so much that I wanted to take him to Manchester City with me but, unfortunately, his reputation away from the treatment room went before him.

He's a top, top man and I love him to bits. Enjoy his story, well at least the parts that he remembers!

SIMPLY THE BEST

'In a flash George had 'nutmegged' all three of us'

I have always loved watching players who excite and thrill. A precious few have the ability to turn a game in a moment. Fortunately, I have worked with some of the very best. Kevin Keegan, Chris Waddle, Peter Beardsley, Paul Gascoigne and Ian Wright spring to mind. The ultimate entertainer of them all made an impression on me before my career had begun.

Like virtually everyone I knew at school I had a dream to make it as a footballer. My hopes began to take shape at the Cliff, Manchester United's training ground in Salford. United were my team and I was one of a group of promising youngsters invited to train at the club during the week. Tuesdays and Thursdays. I was a striker in those days. Come to think of it, weren't we all?! I scored lots of goals but later, beyond school, I was to drop back and make a nuisance of myself in midfield.

The Cliff had an indoor shale pitch and when the weather was bad everyone trained together—the first team, the reserve team, 'A' and 'B' teams. This meant that I was surrounded by all my heroes . . . Denis Law, Bobby Charlton, Pat Crerand and the greatest of them all, George Best. Best was my idol and you can imagine my excitement when I got to play a five-a-side game with him. George was something else. He had everything. His attacking skills were breathtaking and bamboozled defenders but he could also track back and was a great tackler. I looked on in wide-eyed amazement. It was the mid-to late-60s and he was in his pomp.

We used to have a pint of milk and a sandwich afterwards. What impressed me even more was that George would come in and sit with us youngsters. You would not believe it! Bobby Charlton would come over and talk occasionally and others drifted in and out but George was the only one who regularly gave us his time. Me and my mates crowded round and sat there in a trance. We were young and star-struck. There was no big ego here. With a cup of tea in front of him George would chat to us about ordinary, everyday issues. Some of the lads had travelled long distances to get there and George would ask where they were from. He would be particularly supportive to the one or two Irish lads who were in the group.

Many years down the line I was to face the great man once again. I was at Oldham Athletic by then, established as a physiotherapist but keen to get the boots on and have a game whenever possible. I never turned down a chance to play!

It was April 1986 and Oldham manager Joe Royle took a Lancashire Football League team up to Workington to play in a fund-raising match. We had some decent players in the starting line-up, including former Liverpool and England full-back Phil Neal. George turned out for Workington. He flew in and out by helicopter and his picture featured on the front of the match programme. George was a month short of his 40th birthday and well past his peak but he was the star man on the day and his advanced age did not stop him thrilling the crowd.

Our right side midfield player was a lad called Mike Cecere. Mike was decent enough to play around 250 league games, mainly at Oldham, Huddersfield and Walsall. He had the job of keeping George quiet. Not the most enviable of tasks! Mike closed George down on three separate occasions, only to be 'nutmegged' each time. We took Mike to one side and told him how to deal with it, basically to keep his legs tighter together. The fourth time Best approached, Mike did just what we told him. George promptly put the ball one side of him and ran past on the other! Brilliant!

Another Best party piece involved humiliating me! George dribbled towards poor old Mike yet again. I was positioned immediately behind with another of our players behind me. In a flash George had 'nutmegged' all three of us before stopping the ball and running up the touchline with three fingers in the air! You'd think it was staged but I honestly went in to win that ball. I wouldn't shirk a challenge on anyone, even in a friendly, and I've left a few opponents reeling from heavy tackles in my time! With George, I never got close.

Chapter Two

EARLY DAYS

'I was seventeen and gutted'

I was adopted by Hilda and Stan, Mum and Dad, and they made sure that I knew everything from an early age. I couldn't have asked any more from them and loved them both dearly but my antics through my career certainly gave them both plenty of grey hairs! Commenting on something controversial Mum would simply say, 'I don't know where you get it from.'

Sometimes Mum and I didn't speak for up to twelve months because she felt so strongly about my lifestyle. What I got up to was so foreign to her but my attitude was, 'Why are you being upset? This is me. You know what I'm like.' Then I would cool down and realise the error of my ways. Mum had lost a child through an ectopic pregnancy and couldn't have any more so Mum and Dad decided to adopt. They considered doing it a second time but decided that they had enough on with me.

Dad wasn't always happy either but, as a football man himself, he was proud of what I achieved in the game. Recently I went through his desk and found masses of articles about me. Dad used to have an office in his garden in Manchester where he would bash away on the typewriter and smoke non-stop. You could hardly see him when you opened the door!

Mum and Dad, Hilda and Stan

As well as the books and the newspaper work, Dad worked on the Liverpool match programme for twenty-one years. Through his contacts at the club I'd get invites to the big games. I've been to Wembley a couple of times on the back of that connection and used to watch the big European games at Anfield. They were fantastic occasions and I always felt lucky to be involved. I met a lot of people in the game, including players, and attended receptions as well.

One of my best days out was for the 1977 Cup Final between Liverpool and Manchester United. The team that I followed through my Dad against the team I supported. Stuart Pearson, a hero who I later played alongside in some ultra-competitive charity games, opened the scoring for United in the 53rd minute with Jimmy Case replying for Liverpool just two minutes later. I was sitting amongst all the Liverpool followers when Lou Macari's shot deflected off team-mate Jimmy Greenhoff's chest and looped into the goal past Ray Clemence. I jumped up and punched the air before Dad immediately yanked me back down! I was there at Liverpool's expense and he didn't want any trouble!

Despite being offered an apprenticeship at Manchester United, Dad persuaded me to stay on at Sale Grammar School to do my 'O' levels.

United had a policy that they played their apprentices and took a lot on each year so my chance had gone. A lot of my mates got signed up while I carried on with the Tuesday and Thursday sessions in the group known as 'The Amateurs'. However, Everton got in touch. 'Come in on trial and we'll have a look at you.' I went there effectively a year late.

Two things struck me immediately at Everton. The competition for places was massive and my lack of height was going to be a problem. It was the first time I'd been aware of my physical size and it made me wonder whether I was cut out to go all the way.

I moved across from Manchester to Liverpool. Everton put me in digs just off Queen's Road and I claimed expenses. I made my way to Bellefield, the club's training ground, by bus. Mum and Dad then moved to Heswall on the Wirral so I lived with them, taking a bus to Birkenhead, a train under the Mersey, and another bus to the ground. That journey took well over an hour.

I was at Everton for about three months. It wasn't a long time but I learnt a lot. You have to remember that they were the biggest club in the country at the time. It was 1969 and they won the old First Division title by a street in the season I started. In the year above me were future stars like David Johnson, Mick Lyons and Ronnie Goodlass.

The manager was Harry Catterick, one of the club's greatest. Harry won the league twice and the FA Cup in his twelve years and was very much a figure of authority. His office overlooked the training ground. The blinds used to be kept closed but, occasionally, chinks of light came through and we knew that he was keeping his beady eyes on us. Harry Catterick was rarely seen, preferring to leave the work at the coal face to his coaches who did everything.

As you can imagine with such a successful side, every first team player was a legend. I looked after Colin Harvey's boots—we were the same size foot! Unfortunately, that's where the similarities ended! We both played in midfield but whereas Colin built a career on elegance, as one of the 'Holy Trinity' with Alan Ball and Howard Kendall, I was to become more workmanlike and tenacious.

The youngsters had plenty of opportunity to watch their heroes close-up, from the small-sided team games on the park to the massive competition on the table tennis table.

We had a separate changing room from the first team. If you wanted to talk to a first team player you had to knock on their door and wait for someone to answer it. Barge in unannounced and you were putting yourself in all sorts of trouble. There would definitely be a punishment to follow. It's a bit different today because young professionals just wander in and out of dressing rooms. I suppose it's the way attitudes have changed.

The Everton squad was massive. There was a first team, reserves, 'A' team and 'B' team and they would all be playing every Saturday come rain or shine. Saturday was the day. Only certain first team matches and Youth Cup games would take place in midweek. The 'B' team was made up of young apprentices while the 'A' team had older apprentices and young pros. I played mainly 'B' team but did get some 'A' team games as well. Because of the large number on the books it was not unusual for players with first team experience to be alongside us in the 'A' team from time to time. It was a great experience and it was easy to feel that I was on the way to a football career. Occasionally, we would all come together in the afternoons after training and pick teams. This was when the young lads like myself got to play with the seasoned professionals. It was an amazing opportunity but if you made a mistake you were quickly told about it. I remember Alan Ball marching off one day, getting changed and going home. His team weren't winning and he didn't like the young players he had been teamed up with.

Among the mass of players was Joe Royle, a young pro slightly older than me. Joe was one of a large crowd back then but little was I to know what effect he was going to have on my career further down the line. When I went to Oldham Athletic for an interview, he was manager and remembered me from Everton days so I must have made an impact with him at least!

Another player on the books was a Welsh international but he couldn't get games for Harry Catterick and nobody seemed interested in signing him. He went into the gaffer's office one day to discuss things. Catterick reached across for his FA Directory and tossed it in the direction of the player:

'You can't find a club? Well, there's ninety-two in there. Choose one.'

In a dressing room full of characters there was none bigger than goalkeeper Gordon West. Westy ruled in both changing rooms, with the seasoned pros and the young apprentices. He was an outrageous character, always winding people up and one player who regularly copped for it was full back Sandy Brown. After a shower, Sandy would cover himself with talcum powder from those containers which had the big holes in the top. One day Westy emptied the bottle and replaced it with grout which you use for tiling! Sandy poured it all over himself and erupted. He didn't have to think twice about who had done it. 'Westy!!' he roared. Next thing he was chasing Gordon out of the changing rooms and round the training ground, stark naked. And there were houses overlooking on all sides!

Gordon West, Everton legend and massive character

Gordon West was our PFA representative so came round collecting subs from us. Once a month he would put a towel on his head, a book under his arm and head off down to the apprentices. We knew what was coming and the senior players would keep their door open to hear what was about to happen.

Gordon would come in with his book and more often than not we'd all be having a bit of banter. With minimum hand movements, Gordon would control us just like a school teacher with an unruly class. Over and over again he would motion us to stand up, sit down, stand up and sit down. There would be total silence. Another movement with the hand and we would start singing,

'For Westy's a jolly good fellow, for Westy's a jolly good fellow . . . !' or 'Westy's better than Yashin, Westy's better than Yashin, and so say all of us.'

A reference to Lev Yashin, the Russian goalkeeper, who was considered by many to be the greatest in the game's history. Westy would make us sing loud then it was time to shut up again as he started reciting from his book who owed what. He would come down the line, one at a time, and shake us if we wouldn't or couldn't pay.

Every morning I went into training it was like a street market outside. Car boots would be open and there was all sorts for sale. You could buy a joint of beef, fruit, large cans of soup, grapefruit segments and I'm sure a lot of it came off the back of a lorry. There were suit lengths which you would buy and take to Burtons in Liverpool to be made up. I've got two or three. You could design your own. I decided that I wanted a distinctive feature in one of mine.

'You can't have a twenty inch vent,' the assistant said to me.

'I want one,' I replied and got one. I'd put my hands in my pockets and the whole back would open up. I had three pockets on one side on one of the suits. You could have straight pockets, angled pockets. Anything went.

Everton saw my potential and offered me an apprenticeship but I broke my ankle in one of the games. In the end they decided that they were not taking me on but I could stay for the rest of the season. I was seventeen and gutted. Rejection by Everton made me realise that I wasn't going to make it as a footballer. Those dreams I had of running out at Old Trafford and Wembley had been shattered. It had been a wonderful experience to be associated with such a massive club but I had to face reality and decide if I still had it in me to push on at another level in the game

I went up to Blackpool for a short time on an arrangement similar to that at Everton. Blackpool's training pitch at Squires Gate was in between the Pontins holiday camp and the town's airport at the southern end of the seaside resort. We'd be running round the pitch when suddenly an announcement would ring out in the distance,

'Ding, dong, ding, dong, morning campers . . . . the Donkey Derby starts at twelve o' clock!'

Next thing a light aeroplane would circle low from the opposite direction before landing nearby! There was never a dull moment!

Chapter Three

LOOKING FOR A PROPER JOB

'I got a view of the world from above the crossbar!'

My various attempts at breaking into football were clearly not working so I continued my education. I enrolled at West Cheshire College of Further Education at Carlett Park on the Wirral. I studied for my 'A' Levels there and played as an amateur at Blackpool for a while, just turning up for Saturday games. Disciplinary problems plagued me in those early days, a sign of what was to come in my adult career. I was sent off in two games running at Blackpool, for fighting. The opposition were Liverpool and Tranmere Rovers, further embarrassment for Mum and Dad! Blackpool eventually came and went but it wasn't to be the last that I saw of the resort.

Teaching appealed to me and I went to Chester College. I had an interest in sports injuries and got some information about physiotherapy but faced the problem that it was hospital-based and I had a bit of a phobia about hospitals at that time. I remember getting a football injury as a lad and was taken by Dad to a hospital which resembled a workhouse. The experience put me off. Studying physiotherapy meant that I had to attend operations and I couldn't cope with the thought so went into teaching. The phobia seems pretty strange looking back through a career where the significant part of my working life has been linked to injuries and operations!

On leaving college, I got a teaching job at St. Hugh's Roman Catholic Boys School in Birkenhead for five years. You won't find St. Hugh's on the map now. The school closed in the early 1980's and was then demolished. I taught PE which allowed me to keep my interest in sport and I also had time to continue playing football. The school's Head of PE, Ray Leigh, was a friend of mine who helped me get the job. St. Hugh's catered for the poorer families in Birkenhead and the job could be very challenging. One kid disappeared for a while. His mate said, 'He's gone on holiday, sir. He'll be back in about three months.' I guessed he'd been sent to borstal. When he came back I asked him how he was and if he was glad to be home.

'I preferred it in there. I had my own room, watched telly and someone looked after me.'

That said a lot about the sort of life some of the pupils led. Although confined this lad felt safer and happier there than at home. A lot of the kids didn't want to do sport, which didn't help. Despite this, I met the issues head-on, formed a good relationship with most pupils and enjoyed the teaching. There was a really competitive spirit among the kids. They excelled in football and cricket while athletics was introduced by Ray while I was there.

There were mass games lessons in the afternoons and the kids were driven out by bus to playing fields near Tranmere Rovers ground in Birkenhead. The teachers insisted that the pupils travelled downstairs on the double-deckers so they could control them. Reggie McGuire was an exception to that rule. Reggie and a few of his mates ran the school. I didn't have to do any discipline. They sorted the problems out for me. They all loved football and Reggie was already with Tranmere part-time. Reggie would sneak upstairs on the bus and we all knew why! I would follow him up and rather than make a fuss I joined him for a smoke! There were some real hard characters at St. Hugh's. The worst behaved of the lot was also the best player in the football team. He would wag off all the time and we had to tell him he wouldn't play for school, town or county if he kept doing that. Nevertheless, he still went 'over the wall'! Incidentally, Reggie's son, Jamie, was to make his mark in my professional career, as a no-nonsense midfielder at Fleetwood

Town. I rate Jamie very highly. Definitely a chip off the old block and a grand lad!

Despite my lax attitude regarding the smoking on the bus, I must have made a good impression at St. Hugh's because I ended up as Head of Department in the early 1970s. I have to admit, though, that my promotion was helped by Ray Leigh running off with an air stewardess! During this time I was busy in football. I got my first FA coaching qualification, trained the Birkenhead Schoolboys Team and became assistant manager of the Merseyside team. There were some good players to work with, including Peter Davenport, Nigel Adkins, Tommy Caton and Colin Russell. They all went on to make a mark as professionals.

Despite building a career outside the game, I loved football too much to give up playing. Having sampled life right at the top of the football ladder, at Old Trafford and Goodison Park, I was now sampling non-league football as a semi-professional. I started playing in the Welsh League with the likes of Bethesda, Pwllheli and Flint Town. I began as a wide midfield player before going into the middle then, briefly, into the attack at Flint where I played with one of Ian Rush's brothers. Injuries to my knee and ankle limited my games somewhat.

Bethesda: on the back row complete with beard!
Big mate Neil Colbourne is the goalkeeper

I was a semi-professional at Rhyl when Neville Southall was making a name for himself at Winsford United in the Cheshire League. It was the 1979-80 season. I was a feisty midfielder out to make a nuisance of myself which got me my fair share of yellow and red cards. Goalkeepers were a particular target. I was not tall enough to trouble them in the air but the intention was to cause problems from corners. That was my job. I would barge into the keeper and swing my arm across his chest. The immediate reaction when someone nudges you across the chest like that is to pull an arm down and that can be a distraction when you are looking to claim a high ball.

Now Nev was a big boy, even in those early days. He was in his early 20s but had worked as a bin man and a hod carrier in his teenage years. I liked to break forward on occasions into the box. In this particular game, our lad crossed the ball and I tried to get my head to it. I was up against the big man and came off second best. Nev aimed to punch the ball clear and got me. For the first and only time in my football career I got a view of the world from above the crossbar! I hit the ground with a thud, landing on my shoulder and injuring it.

Three goalkeepers of my era hurt me—Terry Gennoe (Blackburn), Mark Wallington (Leicester) and Nev. All went on to a high level. God, I used to hate keepers! It was something that was implanted in my brain. Among other things, they had the licence to come out and hit you with their feet, a tackle which we would have been sent off for in midfield.

Pwllheli celebrate. My hands are firmly in pockets in the second row. Had been subbed and not happy!

Teaching was going well but I never felt that it was going to be my lifetime vocation. I always had an interest in sporting injuries and a yearning to practice physiotherapy so I went to the local library for some ideas. I thought that if I was ever going to do it I should do it now. I saw a three-year course to become a Chartered Physiotherapist and wrote off to Salford School of Physiotherapy. It was based in university but the hospital side was now more appealing because facilities had improved. The practical parts were definitely hospital-based but my thinking was, 'If I see an operation I don't like I can shut my eyes!'

On the face of it, I had little relevant experience. It amounted to Physics 'O' level and what I had done on my PE course. I was awarded a bursary by the DFSS amounting to £50 per week but still needed more funds. There was about £30 per week coming in from my football. Dad had done the Liverpool match programme for over twenty years, including a quiz. He handed it over to me for a little extra cash. A further source of revenue was the Bobby Charlton Soccer Schools. I helped coach on the first ever, at the University of Manchester. I helped out for a couple of years.

I turned my back on teaching and St. Hugh's and soon after the school amalgamated with another down the road. The original buildings were demolished and replaced by housing. They were definitely some happy days for me but I really knew what I wanted to do with my career. Physiotherapy beckoned.

I loved working in the hospitals and my apprehensions were not nearly as bad as I had feared. It was totally different from being a patient. The camaraderie and banter were brilliant. I found that operations fascinated me rather than put me off! I would get closer and closer to the action. One drawback was that I couldn't express a particular interest in sports injuries because I was being paid to train by the NHS. It wasn't set in stone but they preferred you not to specialise but train around each discipline before concentrating on one. As soon as I qualified I wanted to work in football.

The first year, 1979 into 1980 was the hardest of my life. I had six one hour lectures a day! There was some respite on Wednesday with a half day off but they still expected you to read up at home. I would do a couple of hours when I got back but trained on Tuesdays and Thursdays at Pwllheli which was a round trip of about 250 miles. Saturdays frequently found me travelling even further if I was away.

If you failed part one you had to retake the exam and if you failed it a second time you were out. In years two and three you spent half your time at university and half in hospital. I went to see Kevin Murphy the physio at Sale Rugby Club. He said, 'If you want to do it you will but it will be hard.' I always remember his advice and am glad that I stuck by it.

During my third year at Salford I was playing part-time for Flint. I had twisted a knee in pre-season and was in a back splint for six weeks. Although I was training to be a physiotherapist I ignored my own advice and tried to play in October. I played a couple of games and the knee would swell. Having decided it wasn't doing me good I volunteered my services at Tranmere Rovers. They wrote back saying that there wasn't an opening but they would keep me on file. I carried on playing for a while and was pleasantly surprised to hear from them again in December. Eddie Robertson, their physio, had unfortunately dropped dead on the beach during a training session. Manager Bryan Hamilton asked me if I could help as they were coming up to a busy holiday period of games. He intended to have a look at me in action, I could see what life was like at a football club and we could see how it went. There was a familiar face from the past. Gordon West had come out of retirement to play briefly for Rovers but fortunately didn't make me sing for him! I lived just down the road in New Brighton and it coincided with my Christmas break which helped.

Bryan was really good, one of a number of managers who have given me sound advice on life as well as football. He sat me down and said,

'What are you going to do for the rest of your life?'

I replied, 'I want to be a physiotherapist.'

'Well, forget about playing then.'

He was perpetually bubbly, no matter what he was feeling. That was a difficult lesson for me to learn. For a start, I wasn't a morning person. It can also be really hard in the depths of the season. By January you are in to your seventh month, the weather's bad, you've got injuries and at times like that it can be hard to smile. Bryan Hamilton was larger-than-life and quite a wise man. Strict but fair. He got me started so I will always be grateful to him. Getting my foot in the door at Prenton Park was to help propel me into my career in football.

Bryan Hamilton, a great guy who gave me
my first chance in football

The 1982 season ended and I qualified in July. At Tranmere I treated the players, joined in training and did more rehab on my knee. I also got the chance to play with the reserves. I was really enjoying life and would have stayed for the rest of my career. The players weren't all full-time. I had taught some of them! There was John Aspinall and John Kerr, who is sadly not now with us. Nigel Adkins, my keeper in the Town team, was another looking to forge a career in football. He went on to success as a player and a manager. And, of course, there was Reggie McGuire, my smoking partner on the top of the school bus!

Those who had known me as their teacher still called me 'sir'. That soon went out of the window. I told them, 'It's SOSS now.'

Just as things were ticking over nicely and I was getting my feet under the table Bryan came to me one day and said,

'I'm really struggling to get money to pay you so my advice is to start applying for other jobs.'

It wasn't what I wanted to hear but I couldn't begrudge the opportunity that he had given me. I looked around and was offered a job at Walsall. While I was considering that an opportunity came along at Newcastle United. I rang them, having seen the vacancy advertised in a paper that Bryan had shown me. I made some enquiries.

'We expect to give the job to one of five we have already short-listed,' was the not too optimistic message from the north-east.

Chapter Four

KEV AND I ARRIVE ON TYNESIDE

'I'd like you to meet Arfa, your Majesty.'

With a short-list that was far more experienced than anything I could offer I was surprised when Newcastle manager, Arthur Cox, rang me one Saturday morning early in July 1982 to go up for interview. I was in bed in my house in New Brighton at the time of the call but by that afternoon Joy, my wife, and I were at the Newcastle club doctor's house in Sedgefield, a small town in County Durham.

Afterwards we drove back to the in-laws in Pontefract and Arthur rang me, as promised, at nine 'o' clock in the evening. The job was mine and I accepted. I got my first instructions from Arthur,

'Put your house up for sale on Monday and I'll see you at St James' Park first thing on Tuesday morning. Don't forget to bring your passport because you're going to Madeira on Friday for pre-season training.'

Bloody hell! Things were moving fast. In the blink of an eye I had gone from £5 a week in a part-time capacity to a full-time job at one of the biggest clubs in the land. It was a massive step-up. Although Newcastle were in Division Two at the time there was, in every other respect, a Division One set-up. They had finished the 1981-82 season in ninth position, some twenty-six points behind champions Luton Town.

Joy was established as a teacher in a local primary school on the Wirral but knew that I was ambitious and that this was my big chance. She was prepared to sacrifice what she had for me to pursue this brilliant opportunity. I had been the outsider coming up on the rails to beat more experienced candidates and, looking back, I soon realised that Arthur Cox was a man who liked to be in control and perhaps he saw me as someone he could mould. I was the novice, starting out with a lot to learn.

Just three days after making the journey up for interview I was on the training ground with the Newcastle United first team. The Tuesday session was followed by others on Wednesday and Thursday. Then I was at the ground bang on time on the Friday, bound for the island of Madeira. I looked around as the players gathered but there was no sign of Arthur. Tommy Cavanagh, his assistant, was nearby. Tommy was a Scouser and a really big character who had got himself into trouble for swearing on a number of occasions in his career, not least when working alongside Tommy Docherty at Manchester United. Sadly, he passed away from Alzheimer's disease in 2007. I asked him where the gaffer was and he replied,

'He's signing Kevin Keegan. It's a fucking joke.'

Tommy couldn't believe it, and neither could I, but a few miles away from where we were standing Arthur Cox was about to reveal one of the biggest signings in Newcastle United's history. The news capped a pretty amazing week in my life.

Madeira was an early opportunity for me to get to know the players. There wasn't much difference between us age-wise and we shared similar interests. I went out with them most nights. I liked a few drinks and just couldn't resist the chance to get out on the town. Tommy Cavanagh had slapped a curfew of eleven o'clock on the lads. My room was on the first floor. Somehow they found a ladder which they placed up to my balcony and I would leave the door open for them. Cav never found out and I'm guessing that it might not have appealed to the management but it helped me to bond quickly with the players. It amuses me how things have changed through my career. From being a similar age to the players back in the mid-80s, I have become more like a father-figure, even grandfather-figure in recent years!

The Keegan deal was done while we were in Madeira and by the time we got back to Tyneside Keegan-mania had already hit the city. Fans were swarming around for a glimpse of the great man and queuing for tickets. Kevin Keegan had arrived and he transformed the fortunes of Newcastle United and the city itself.

By the time he arrived in the north-east, Keegan had made his name. After three years at Scunthorpe United, he had flourished under Bill Shankly at Anfield where he scored just twelve minutes into his debut, against Nottingham Forest. Between 1971 and 1977 he formed a lethal partnership with John Toshack and won three League titles, one FA Cup, two UEFA Cups and a European Cup. He then became one of the English game's biggest names abroad, the highest paid player in Germany as part of a Hamburg side which took the title for the first time in nineteen years. European Footballer of the Year Awards in 1978 and 1979 were followed by another European Cup final. His move to Newcastle followed a two-year spell at Southampton which ended with a fall-out with manager Lawrie McMenemy. Kevin signed for Newcastle for a fee of £100 000. The top players today are getting over double that a week!

Kevin's glittering career at club and international level guaranteed that his was no ordinary signing and so it turned out. His passionate following and magic on the pitch ensured that he became an instant hero in a part of the world where they worship footballing gods such as Jackie Milburn, Malcolm Macdonald and Alan Shearer.

Amidst all this hype and excitement, a young physiotherapist from Manchester had slipped in to the club. It was an amazing time for me to be joining United. I pinched myself to make sure that this was all actually happening. Only a few weeks ago, I had been on the Wirral, happy in my first position at Tranmere Rovers. Now I was caught up in a tide of emotion at one of the biggest clubs in the land.

I got to know Kevin Keegan very well and he made a big impact on me, both as a player and as a man. He organised shooting practices after training. There would be two wingers, a striker and no goalkeeper. Kevin would play the ball out wide, advance down the middle to meet the cross and, with one touch, finish the move. Sometimes he would volley, sometimes half-volley, maybe there would be a header. He would have ten attempts altogether, five from the left and five from the right. Kevin regularly scored seven times. You would think that without a keeper in position it should be more. Well, Newcastle's other strikers would go through the same ritual and score two or three times. I used to love watching him do that routine.

Kevin started alongside Imre Varadi, a good striker who could score you twenty goals a season. Varadi had bagged a few in his first season at St. James' Park and linked well with another Tyneside legend, Chris Waddle. Imre was a journeyman who appeared for something like sixteen clubs at all levels of English football. He rarely spent more than two years at one place and never made a hundred appearances for any single club. After Kevin joined, Imre's total for the second season went up to twenty-one goals. Come the end of that season, Kevin said,

'OK, Varadi has scored twenty-one goals this season. I've set him up to score sixty. How many times has he set me up? None. Fact.' Varadi moved on yet again.

By and large, the players at Newcastle weren't as good as those that Kevin had played with and a lot of the delivery he received might best be described as fighting balls, tossed into the air, hit and hope and needing a headed challenge. This happened particularly in his first year at St. James' Park but when he was eventually joined by others of the calibre of Peter Beardsley and Chris Waddle things improved. Although he was often likely to get clattered by a big centre half, Kevin never shirked a challenge. Always a marked man, he was the most courageous of players. There was never a complaint.

I remember the time we kept an injury quiet. We were due on the plastic pitch at Queen's Park Rangers and Kevin's ankle was three times the size it should have been. He refused to even put his foot in the ice-bucket. He said he would just go out and play. We lost 3-0 and he was just at half pace. He got a right slating off the London press but didn't make excuses.

Off the field, Kevin did a lot of work for the brewery who paid part of his wage. He was also sponsored by sportswear company Patrick and men's fragrance Brut. He would always be using their brand new gear and samples at the training ground. There would be regular visits to my room at the end of a training session where he would say,

'You are about my size, SOSS, help yourself to some stuff.'

Keegan came in one day. He told me that he had something on the back seat of his car for me. It was a giant Wurlitzer jukebox, an all-singing, all-dancing model.

'Wow, Kev,' I said, 'I've always wanted one of those.'

'You can have it for £300. I've got one, you can have the other.'

I told him that there was no way I could afford to pay for it. I was on about £30 a week at the time. He suggested I take it anyway and let me have the money when I got it.

'But I'd be owing you for it forever,' I said. As much as I wanted one I had to decline the offer. Kevin's generosity extended beyond his period at Newcastle. When he headed off to Spain in temporary exile he bought all the lads and everyone at the club a going-away present.

Keegan used to give me wads of cash to look after during matches. I would ask him how much and he would never know. I'd ask him to count it so that I wasn't doing him out of any cash but he would simply say,

'Don't worry, mate, I trust you. Just look after it.'

£300 was just loose change to him. He never flaunted his money, though. I was often the brunt of Keegan's sense of humour. We used to stay in the Tower Hotel when in London and Willie McFaul and I would arrange to have a few drinks. Willie was a smashing bloke who served Newcastle as player, coach, assistant manager and manager. There was one occasion when I had been up most of the night having a few drinks and the lads must have got wind of this. Keegan went down early in the game at Chelsea the next day. He lay at virtually the furthest point from the dug-out. When I got across to him there was a big smile across his face,

'Look at the state of him, ref. He looks like he's been up all night drinking and he can't even run in a straight line. You're zig-zagging all over the place, SOSS. All he has to do is breathe on you and it makes you get up.' It was a joke at my expense which had obviously been planned.

Then there was the time when he had the rest of the team in stitches when we were on tour, introducing me to the King of Thailand as 'Arfa'. It was an end-of-season Far Eastern tour and Arthur Cox had named me as one of the substitutes. Both teams were introduced to the King on the pitch before the game and when His Majesty arrived in front of me, Kevin, who was captain, said,

'I'd like you to meet Arfa, your Majesty.'

The King replied, 'Pleased to meet you, Arfa' and the rest of the lads fell about laughing. How do you explain to the King of Thailand that I was called Arfa because Kevin always claimed that I looked like Tom Selleck, who played television private investigator Magnum, but I was only half his size!

Kev and 'Arfa'!

Kevin embraced the north-east, moving into the area to live rather than be based hundreds of miles away like many professionals do today. He was an all-action hero, all go, a great role model. His quality as a player was still in evidence and, in my opinion, he hasn't been appreciated as much as he should have been.

A lot of actors, comedians and singers traditionally supported the club and would come to games, particularly if they were performing in the city. More came after Keegan arrived. There would be the likes of Mark Knopfler from 'Dire Straights', and lads such as Jimmy Nail and Tim Healey from the popular TV programme 'Auf Wiedersehen, Pet'.

Freddie Starr came into the changing room once. Arthur Cox was a tough taskmaster but let it happen. Starr was talking seriously to the lads before the game and I was willing him to do or say something funny. We had large, sunken baths at the club in those days. We would start filling them with cold water then add the hot from half time. It was getting half-full with cold when I noticed Freddie talking to our goalkeeper about making diving saves. He edged nearer to the bath. Suddenly he leapt full stretch to one side and landed in the bath! Hilarious! He must have been thinking about how he could put a smile on the lads' faces and that was his answer.

As well as his contacts in show business, Kevin had a massive interest in horse racing. He used to ring the jockeys up from my room. There would be Pat Eddery in the Flat Season and Jonjo O'Neill over the jumps. He was really into it big style. For a short period we had Mick Channon with us on loan. He was another amazing character and made his way in horse racing as a top trainer. Mick used to swear like a trooper with a broad West Country drawl. We were in this posh hotel in London and Mick was swearing like mad. He was one of those people who never sounded offensive when he was swearing. A bloke came up and said,

'Would you keep the swearing down, please? I'm with my wife.'

Mick replied, quick as a flash, 'She'd rather hear me than be deaf wouldn't she?' The bloke didn't have an answer and wandered off shaking his head. We creased ourselves.

Welsh jockey Neale Doughty won the 1984 Grand National with Hello Dandy. Neale was a big Newcastle fan and was massive friends with Kevin and Terry McDermott. When Neale was injured his friends stepped in, inviting him to Newcastle for treatment. There was already a two-inch screw in his shoulder from a previous accident but I soon had him back in action and he was very grateful.

'Now I want Newcastle to win promotion so I can celebrate a great double!' said the Grand National winner.

Neale wasn't the only example of me being involved in a different sport. British number one tennis player, Buster Mottram, had to withdraw from a tennis tournament he had dominated for the last two years. A knee problem was proving to be very painful. I treated him and diagnosed tendonitis.

Kevin left for retirement at the end of the 1983-84 season, having scored 48 goals in 78 games for Newcastle. I well remember a game that was instrumental in helping him make the decision to retire. It was a Third Round FA Cup tie against his beloved Liverpool at Anfield on a Friday night in January 1984. We had stopped over at Haydock Park for rest time during the afternoon. The lads went to bed to get some rest but Kevin was never a big fan of that. Quite by chance, Haydock Park races were on and four of us walked across some fields to the course. There was Kevin, myself, Terry Mac and one other whose name I can't remember. We arrived at the back end of the course in time to see the horses go by. We leaned on the fence and watched. Jonjo O'Neill comes past. He obviously saw Kevin and on the next lap he shouted across to us, 'I don't fancy this one today!' Keegan had money on him as well!

Liverpool were in the old First Division and on the way to their third successive league title, we were still in the Second. On paper we had no right to beat them and eventually went down 4-0. Ian Rush bagged a couple I seem to remember. Kevin was put through on one occasion and I think it was Alan Hansen who took five yards out of him in the space of ten yards before taking the ball off him. Kevin stood in the middle of the pitch with his hands on his hips for what seemed like an eternity, in disbelief. It was probably only thirty seconds or so but it seemed like much longer. He was stunned that someone had done that to him. At the end of the game Kevin sat in the dressing room and wouldn't take his kit off so that I could pack it away with the rest. I couldn't persuade him. Not a word was spoken. I could tell that he had realised in his own mind that he couldn't hack it at the top level any more.

A few days after the end of the 1983-84 campaign, Liverpool were again the opposition as Newcastle staged a friendly at St. James' Park. It was Kevin's last game and, after it, he was flown away by helicopter. We all went to the Gosforth Park Hotel at the Newcastle Racecourse. Kevin had bought everyone presents and it was clear that he had put some thought into it. I got a leather document holder which was really nice. Kevin went in to management and returned to Newcastle in 1992, almost eight years after his final game as a player. The proud club was sliding and his appointment was an attempt to prevent it from being relegated into the third tier of English football for the first time. He made an impact off the field as he had on it a decade earlier and gained the adoring nickname 'King Kev' from his devoted fans. Eventually, he got the top job as England's manager and everywhere he went he took Arthur Cox with him. Cox had given him one last big opportunity as a player and Keegan had not let him down. Arthur was hard and uncompromising. It took the influence of Keegan to mellow him. Sometimes Kevin would say, 'You can't do that, boss.' It had an effect and Arthur became better for it. Keegan brought laughter into the club. He was like a breath of fresh air around St. James' Park.

Kevin Keegan timed his departure from Newcastle United perfectly as the club he had transformed returned to the top flight, finishing in third place behind Chelsea and Sheffield Wednesday. There was a feeling around that we were heading for promotion, particularly with results away from home. It was entertainment week-in, week-out and between them the likes of Keegan, Beardsley and Waddle hammered in 85 goals. There were some fantastic performances over the two years. I particularly remember Barnsley, never an easy place to go to. We annihilated them 5-0 in May 1983. If you could get results like that anything was possible because you were very lucky to get anything from Oakwell. Mick McCarthy was around at that time and they had two big centre halves that looked like bank robbers! You rarely got anything out of them but with Kevin Keegan as the catalyst anything was possible.

Amidst all this excitement, my feet barely touched the ground in those early weeks and months on Tyneside. Joy had given a term's notice and left her primary school at Christmas 1982. I had started in digs in Killingworth, a town north of the city, and as Joy joined me in the area we bought a brand new house in Wallsend, an area which derives its name as the location at the end of Hadrian's Wall. In the absence of a teaching post being available Joy went to work for a friend who had a pub in Eldon Square in the city centre. Our first son, James, came along soon after.

I used to think that Newcastle was like a separate territory. I'd never been that far north in my life, even to visit. Leeds was the next big place in my eyes while my home town of Manchester seemed worlds away! The locals were a breed apart in the north-east, passionate about football, cricket, racing, greyhounds and pigeons. It could be a bleak area in the winter. It got dark earlier. We had a dog and took it for walks but didn't see many people during the long winter months.

Chapter Five

THE GAFFER

'There are a hundred physiotherapists out there who could do your job.'

It is fair to say that I had never experienced anyone quite like Arthur Cox. Arthur was an extremely intense person, 100% committed to football. That was his life. He broke his leg playing in a reserve game for Coventry City and had to retire at a young age. He worked under Bob Stokoe as a coach at Sunderland, learning his trade from one of the legendary managers. As early as day two of my time on Tyneside Arthur told me to forget about playing football. He knew my history and saw me knocking the ball around. Having played at Tranmere Rovers this came as a shock. I was passionate about playing and it crossed my mind for a moment that I might have made a mistake. I had to push him for a reason, that's in my nature. His reply was, 'Who will treat you when you are injured?'

I can be a stubborn fella at times. Killingworth had a working men's club with a Sunday League side. It was a good standard and, despite Arthur's wishes, I played for them. I formed a few friendships and then also played midweek floodlit football in the Northern League for Whitley Bay out on the coast. Around this time I became mates with Jim Pearson, a striker at Everton and Newcastle. Jim was playing for Gateshead and I went along to join in, giving a bit of help physio-wise.

Arthur eventually discovered my new friendship and immediately tried to ban me from seeing Jim.

Arthur was funny that way. He didn't trust anyone, even the club's directors. He would say to me,

'Think on, one day these people will be sat round a table discussing your future.'

This was sound advice which I was to pass on to others through my career. One of my jobs was to answer the phone for Arthur at Benwell training ground. He had the next room to mine. If anyone wanted the gaffer, I couldn't say he was in even if I knew he was. I always had to 'go and have a look for him'. I would pop my head round the door of his office and say,

'Jack Charlton's on the phone, boss.'

Arthur would sit with his hand on his chin looking out of the window for what seemed like an age. I sometimes had to repeat what I'd just said. The reply eventually came back,

'Tell him I'm not in, he's after my job.'

That reply applied to a few of those who rang, not just Jack. Eventually, it got to the stage where I would go back to the phone and say,

'He's told me to tell you that he's not in!'

Arthur also used to have me on sentry duty at the training ground gates to stop reporters getting in. I was quite friendly with the press and it was in their interest to be friendly with me because Arthur was so difficult to deal with. I guess they were trying to get information out of me in the absence of the manager and I had to be careful. So I'd stand with a smile on my face and say something like,

'Now then, lads, Arthur has decreed that you be banned from training today. What have you lot been doing to upset him?'

There was never any trouble. Because the club was such a focal point in the city and it was like living in a goldfish bowl Arthur was all too aware that stories easily got out so he didn't want any outsiders involved. 'They'll be straight to the press,' he would say. Jim Pearson was one such example in the manager's eyes but I didn't think it was Arthur's place to tell me who I mixed with and carried on seeing Jim anyway.

I got sent off playing for Whitley Bay against Tow Law. The referee did me for foul language. The following night I was back page headlines in the Chronicle. I was summoned by Arthur the next morning and was expecting a bollocking. He delivered one and told me once again not to play. I got a few roastings around that time because I was young and rebellious. Arthur would tell me,

'There are a hundred physiotherapists out there who could do your job.'

I'd reply, 'Go and get them and see if they are as good as me.'

He wasn't going to dictate to me. My playing instinct surfaced again and I went back to Whitley Bay, realising that I had to tow the line. The repercussions of that sending-off could have been very awkward for me because the FA got involved. They said that I could be banned from doing my work as Newcastle's physio. Fortunately, it did not come to that. Returning to the club was a risky strategy but I couldn't resist the urge to play.

Midweek leagues were popular for shift workers and unemployed and as I got Wednesday afternoons off there was always the opportunity to play a game or two. One team I played for was featured in a picture in the paper with some medals we won and I deliberately hid behind the guys in front so that no-one recognised me!

Despite Arthur's wish to stop me playing, I would be treating someone at a training session when an apprentice would come in saying,

'Get your boots on, Arthur needs you to play outside.' My reply was always, 'Tell him he's banned me from playing!'

The apprentice would run backwards and forwards between us! I always said it tongue-in-cheek because in the end I never passed up the chance to play. Kevin Keegan once put in a book,

'It's a poor state of affairs when your physio's your best player!'

I'd probably marked him out of a training game! It didn't matter what type of game I was in, I always gave it my all. The lads used to like it when I went in goal. I was all over the place, diving, getting muddy, trying to cope with my lack of height.

Arthur could be difficult to work with. Irish international, Mick Martin, was recovering from an injury and I remember him once telling me to put black boot polish on a white bandage. Newcastle United wore black shorts and the injury would stand out less. I put the 'black' bandage on Mick's torn thigh but made it clear to Arthur that in my opinion he wasn't fit and Arthur risked losing him. Mick played and 'bang' he did the thigh again—out for a month. One of the directors pulled me after the game and said,

'Whose idea was that? Was it Arthur's?'

I had to agree.

He replied, 'I thought so'.

Despite our differences Arthur and I were fairly close. The boss was alright under that stern, gruff exterior. Looking back I could see that he was trying to guide me in the best way he could. To be fair to him, he always looked after me. I got into a few scrapes and he stood by me, no matter what. That is something that I will never forget. He did put in writing in an article one day that, 'Ian Liversedge is like a son to me.'

You had to be really careful in the city. I have already mentioned the time when we got beat by Liverpool at Anfield in the FA Cup, the game in which Kevin Keegan began to realise that his end was in sight. Despite this defeat, the Newcastle fans were still making the most of the occasion and were doing the conga behind the goal. I was in a working men's club for a drink later that weekend. I went to the toilet and was sharing a joke with someone. Another punter turned on me and said,

'What you laughing at? You got beat 4-0 yesterday.' That's how serious they were about their football.

I have pointed out his insecurities and foibles but Arthur Cox taught me more about life in two years than anyone. One thing he cautioned against was going out socially with players. He taught me loads about players, the other side of them. I didn't necessarily want to act on his advice at the time because of my closeness to the players age-wise and our shared interests but I heeded his words at other clubs later in my career. It was Tommy Cavanagh who once said about players, 'They'll take the milk out of your tea and come back for the sugar.'

There was a clear message that they could not be trusted and this was Arthur's viewpoint as well. It was a great line from Tommy and I laughed at the time but over the years you learn that players can be very selfish. They only think about themselves then throw you by the wayside when they no longer need you. Life as a professional footballer is like no other. There are twenty or thirty guys living in each other's pockets for ten months of the year. They travel together, train together, eat together. They have everything done for them. A sneeze and they are packed off to the doctor, a problem with an ankle and it's off for a scan. They are taken there and back so they don't have to think about travel. It's a life-style that can easily encourage selfishness and I have seen it so often. Not all are like this, I should add, there are many I respect. Also, I'm sure I've used people as stepping stones to further my own career.

Arthur had massive strength of character and utter belief in what he did. 'Score more goals than the opposition,' was his mantra. It was all about entertainment. Four three rather than one nil. He had a belief in how football should be played and was well-aware of what the Toon Army demanded. They always had to have that star player who they could worship. It took Arthur a while to achieve it but eventually he got it with Kevin Keegan.

Chapter Six

THE GREAT ENTERTAINERS

'Peter Beardsley was capable of doing anything'

I would have considered myself fortunate to watch Kevin Keegan alone from the bench but to have not one but three great stars on show was just plain greedy! Peter Beardsley and Chris Waddle were to grace many a football stage. Waddle, Beardsley and Keegan as a combination were the best I've seen at close quarters and worked with. They were unbelievable and to watch them in action was a joy.

Peter Beardsley was a Hexham lad and a product of the famous Wallsend Boys Club in North Tyneside. He finally settled at St. James' Park after spells with Carlisle United and Vancouver Whitecaps. Peter loved playing football and eating sweets in equal measure! There was always a bag in his pocket! He had unbelievable talent and could do things on a football pitch that others just dreamt about. I saw him chip Manchester City's six foot four goalkeeper, Eric Nixon, from the edge of the penalty area at St. James' Park. No mean achievement and I can't think of many others who would have tried it.

Peter knew what he was going to do with the ball before it arrived and was often not one but two steps ahead of the rest. Whereas many players are restricted by their ability, Peter was capable of doing anything. Football is all about making choices and players of Peter's quality invariably made the right choices. Grass roots players, by contrast, often make the wrong choices. They will run when they should pass or take a touch when they should knock it off. One of Peter's real strengths was that he was unselfish and he took as much delight in bringing others in to play as scoring himself. He scored over a hundred goals in the black and white shirt but created many more. What he did on match days was no fluke. He was always doing those things in training.

Peter was also a fantastic help to me. We had to load the skips with kit before and after games. It wasn't the most pleasant of tasks, particularly after you'd lost, but Peter would always come and help to do it as well as get the stuff back on to the coach after the game.

I remember a time Willie McFaul and I packed for Peter's old team, Carlisle United, on New Year's Day. We rolled up at Brunton Park and realised we had forgotten to include the socks! Willie and I looked at each other as if to say, 'Who the hell's going to tell Arthur?' We decided instead to ask Carlisle if they had a spare set. The good news was that they did and were prepared to lend them but they were red. Well, there's no way that any Newcastle team could wear that colour because of the strong association with Sunderland. The fans would go mad. In the end, we took our lives in our hands and told Arthur whose reply was,

'Well, you're just going to have to play without.'

Willie went out and got hold of the local Yellow Pages. He found the number of a sportswear shop in Carlisle, rang it and, fortunately, the owner lived above the shop. Willie hopped into a taxi, went round and got us twelve pairs.

These days, I'm surprised that clubs don't employ Pickfords to transport their stuff. There seems to be a massive amount of gear and ever more skips full of training bibs, medical kit and the kitchen sink.

Peter Beardsley was totally immersed in his job, a football man through and through. He joined Newcastle in 1983, by which time Chris Waddle had become a firm favourite. Another local lad, Waddle could play off both feet and beat you either way. After my first pre-season trip to

Madeira we went to Scotland for some games. They hated us but it was a good time to do pre-season because they were ahead of us fitness-wise as their season started before ours. The games were always physical. I think it was at Kilmarnock on one occasion where Waddler, to give him his nickname, looked as if he had a sack of coal on his back. He was trudging backwards and forwards with head down. I commented as such to Tommy Cavanagh and suggested Chris came off because he looked done in. Tommy replied,

'Don't worry, mate, he always looks like that. You just wait. He lures defenders in by letting them think he's knackered.'

Sure enough, Chris suddenly sprung to life and left them for dead. He was big, strong and could pass a player on either side with a drop of the shoulder. Chris was not lightning fast but for a big lad he had so much skill.

On another occasion we forgot to pack Chris's boots for a game at QPR. We had to go and find a pair of size tens. Their ground was a mud bath at the time and all we could come back with was a pair with rubber-moulded studs. Arthur insisted that players wore proper studs. I would have been devastated to play on such a pitch with rubbers but Waddle said, 'They're all right' and proceeded to show us what extraordinary balance he had. He never slipped once. When I was training to be a PE teacher we had to define skill. We came up with, 'making the difficult look easy.' That was Chris Waddle in a nutshell.

Chris wasn't too keen on sharing his thoughts with others, though! After games, the press would hang around looking for players for interviews. Chris would be away, out of the fire door and across the car park, often half-dressed! He didn't want to know and this is all the more surprising considering that he has now transformed himself and become a respected and experienced radio and television pundit.

Chris was big mates with Steve Carney and would be regularly dropped off on the A1 having got changed on the coach on the way back north after matches. Then it was over a fence and across a couple of fields to a working-men's club they frequented. These two were really well in to the north-east culture. They used to follow a live band around the pubs and clubs. Steve was a lovely Geordie lad who had come to United from non-league Blyth Spartans just up the road. He played 134 times for the Magpies over six years. An electrician by trade he was a tremendous competitor and a no-nonsense defender. His death from pancreatic cancer in 2013 came as a massive shock.

As for Chris, the Felling-born lad who we never thought would leave the north-east proved us wrong when he moved to Tottenham then Olympic Marseille. He became a massive hit in the south of France and was voted the second best Marseille player of the century in 1998 behind Jean Pierre Papin. He extended his game by developing beautiful long passes and could play either side of a 4-4-2 formation. To get over homesickness he watched recordings of magician Paul Daniels on VHS, leading to the fans nicknaming him 'Magic Chris.' Chris Waddle had a few magic tricks of his own every match day!

As if there wasn't already enough excitement around the club, Newcastle signed a local lad by the name of Paul Gascoigne as an apprentice in 1983. The precocious teenager was looked after by Colin Suggett, the Youth Team manager. On certain afternoons Colin would organise games at the training ground for his lads. I played on one side and Colin played on the other. As with George Best some fifteen years earlier you could see close-up that Gazza was something different. He did amazing things for his age. His had not been a straightforward childhood. He was a street lad, a latch-key kid, with a staple diet of chocolate, crisps and chips. Gazza had come through a system of boys clubs which unearthed a lot of talent and had trials with other clubs before signing for his local team just a few miles from where he grew up in Gateshead.

Newcastle set about sorting Gazza's diet out and the training was strict. There would be games on Saturday mornings at the training ground. If we were at home that day first team players would turn up just to watch Gazza play. For half an hour he would be unbelievable, then he would start to go bright red and look as if he had diver's boots on! The youth games with Leeds United were always worth watching as Gazza came up against another outstanding midfield talent in Scott Sellers. Gazza tore Sellers to pieces for the first half hour or so. He physically dominated him, 'nutmegged' him and showed a quality of passing which you just wouldn't expect from a kid of that age. Then he would go redder and redder, fade from the game and Sellers took over. Eventually Gazza was transformed into a ninety-minute player who could take the game by the scruff of the neck and win it for you. Not many can do that. Like all the great players, Paul knew what he was doing with the ball before it arrived. He had a kind of sixth sense.

I laid Gazza out once in the gym. He had come in a bit strong and I went high and clattered into him! It was just instinct kicking in with me. I didn't go out to injure him deliberately. I thought that Colin wouldn't invite me to take part again. He wouldn't want a competitive rough diamond harming his prized possession! Instead, Colin came over and gave Gazza a telling off,

'How many times have I told you not to do something like that because you'll come up against players like SOSS who is experienced and knows his way round a football pitch.'

I met up with Gazza again at Burnley when he came on loan at the end of his career. His opening shot was, 'Remember when we played the firemen?' We had taken a youth team to play the local brigade in a seven-a-side game. I went along in case things got a bit rough. You knew you were in for a tough game with opposition like that. They were physical and out to get their moment of glory. It was done deliberately to toughen the lads up and you could see who had the bottle and who didn't. It still happens today. Men against boys but a great experience all the same. Suggy ended up putting me on because the fire brigade were going through our lads. I toughened things up a bit and must have done about three of them!

There were clearly signs of the troubled side of Paul Gascoigne at Burnley. He arrived towards the end of the 2001-02 season and had recently spent time in Arizona at an alcoholic rehabilitation centre. He was reliant on a battery of pills and potions to get him through the day. He took diet pills and shed weight. In fact, he had a car boot full of tablets. Despite that, Gazza was still the best player in training by far. The pitches were smaller which helped him and he was unbelievable in five-a-side games.

He shone in training where the pitches were smaller but just couldn't cover the distance any more. He made just six appearances for the first team. Against Sheffield United he kept controlling the ball and looking up to distribute. The opposition were running back and just as he was about to pass they nicked the ball off him. Stan substituted him at half time. I looked on thinking, 'That's probably it now.'

Gazza was so generous he would literally give you the shirt off his back. After matches, he would be surrounded by a clamour of people, all keen to attract his attention. I've seen him take his tracksuit top and shirt off, sign the shirt, give it to a fan and put his top back on. He saw me in a hotel bar when he was with Spurs and I was with Oldham. He came over and handed me his car keys.

'Have a look on the back seat and take what you want, mate.'

There was all sorts of sponsored stuff like signed balls and shirts.

'You can auction them off.'

I replied, 'Very kind of you, mate, but who wants an autographed Spurs shirt in Manchester!' He laughed with that big, broad grin. I'm sure that he learned this generous side of his nature from Kevin Keegan.

At Turf Moor, the mischievous side of his character was still very much in evidence. On Fridays we had a court session. All the misdemeanours of the week were brought up and both staff and players were involved. There would be a £2 fine, perhaps £5 if it was serious. The money went into a pot and was shared out when the lads went on their end of season trip.

Gazza had made a big pot of tea and was insisting people had some. We got on with the court meeting. Gazza got fined and said,

'I don't care really, I've put farting powder in that tea!'

His big mate Jimmy 'Five Bellies' was always with him. The first day Gazza came to training I got to the training ground at a quarter to nine.

Gazza and Jimmy were already there. I asked them why they were so early. Gazza said he'd been there since eight o' clock. I told him that we always went to the ground first, then on to training.

'I couldn't sleep, I wanted to go to the gym,' he replied. He found sleeping difficult and had medication to help him with that as well. He looked like a nervous wreck but Jimmy was a good lad and constantly there to look after his mate.

Gazza would have a few brandies before a game and by the time he was at Burnley he was smoking heavily as, well. He loved playing and when he could no longer do it, it affected him greatly. His problems have been well-documented. A lot of players struggle to cope after retirement and Gazza's is a classic case. He nicknamed me 'The Fizz'. I think that 'physiotherapist' was too long a word for him! Quite a guy and one hell of a player.

Chapter Seven

OUT ON THE TOON

'I opened the door and my room was totally empty'

It was at Newcastle where I developed my passion for having a good time with the booze and the partying. The drinking often started on the team coach coming back north from away games. We started with fish and chips then cracked open the beers. That's all taboo now. There are no fish and chips and definitely no beer on coaches. We would frequently arrive back late at night and I often used to stagger off when we arrived back at St. James' Park, fumbling for what seemed like forever with the keys as I tried to open the big gates to let the coach in. The lads would be shouting,

'Come on! What you playing at? We want to go out.'

In the mid-80's, players would also play Tuesdays and then go out knowing there was a day off Wednesday. The city had a cracking night-life and I was intending to enjoy it to the full. Arthur Cox didn't like me going out with the lads but I did. One of those who loved a night out was Terry McDermott.

Keegan, Waddle and Beardsley weren't the only legends at St. James' Park. Terry McDermott was right up there with them. My God, what a character! The England midfielder was in his second spell at the club.

After a season or so under Joe Harvey in the mid-seventies, Terry moved to Liverpool and made his name over the next eight years with twenty-five England caps as well.

Terry arrived back on Tyneside when I went up there and he was an absolute star, one of the funniest people that I've ever met. He had to miss two weeks on one occasion when he hit a snowplough in his car! Terry loved life to the full. Now, I liked my drink but even I found it difficult to keep up with Terry Mac! Terry was one of those rare footballers who had as much an appetite for drinking as he did for training. He could drink all night then come in the next day and lead the way. I'm convinced he had hollow legs.

Terry's training regime showed when he was recovering from injury once and I took him out to the coast at Whitley Bay. We went for a run up the beach, a couple of miles perhaps. We had done the first half and had turned back. There was a player called Neil McDonald with us. Neil was yet another former Wallsend Boys Club product, joining Newcastle as an apprentice and playing over two hundred games at right-back and in midfield. He was very one paced but could run all day. Anyway, out on the beach at Whitley Bay, Terry let Neil get about a hundred yards ahead then launched himself after him and beat him back. When I caught up with them Terry was already setting up markers for shuttle runs and ran Neil into the ground. He had unbelievable stamina and was out the night before as well!

All the sides I've had success with have had an element of fun and Terry was one of those who could always put a smile on your face. I don't think you can survive in any industry without a laugh. At Newcastle there used to be plenty and he was usually at the heart of it.

One place favoured by the players was the Tuxedo Junction, a popular nightclub. It had telephones on the tables which allowed you to chat people up across the room! One night this girl at the bar made a complaint about Terry. In training the following day I got called into Arthur's office, which was next to mine. I hated getting the summons. It was always a cloak and dagger approach with Arthur. On this particular day he told me to bring McDermott straight in and he told me why.

When Terry arrived I told him that the gaffer wanted to see him about the bird at the bar last night. Terry couldn't remember a thing. Arthur asked me to stay in for the meeting so there we were like two naughty schoolboys in front of the headmaster. Arthur spelt out the tale before asking Terry what he had to say.

'It's like this boss,' replied Terry, 'When I stay on the pints I'm ok but when I go on the wine I don't know what I'm doing.'

I'm thinking, 'Fucking hell, Terry, talk about digging a big hole for yourself, mate.'

It seemed like an age before the gaffer spoke. Arthur sat, as ever, with his chin in his hands and stared out of the window. The reply eventually came back,

'In future, Terry, just stay on the pints.'

After we went out Terry kept asking me, 'What the fuck was I doing?'

'Just keep walking, mate, before you get in to even more trouble.'

Thirty years on it has become so much more difficult for players to enjoy themselves in the clubs and pubs like they did in my time at Newcastle. Everyone has mobile phones with cameras in these days and with Twitter and Facebook every move can be recorded. Players have become so much more vulnerable and some in recent times have got themselves into massive trouble as complaints have come in about them. Suddenly your whole career is threatened. Also, the game has got far more serious at the top level and players just don't party as much as they used to. I blame the Sky and Premier League revolution a lot for all that.

Terry played cards a lot with Kevin. They were like chalk and cheese as characters but fantastic friends. They gelled together and bounced off each other. They were later to become manager and assistant at Newcastle. Some years later I met up with Terry in a pre-season game between Fleetwood Town and Huddersfield. He hadn't changed, still a lovely lad.

I remember an end of season Far East tour which was just one big piss up for twenty-two days and at the end of it we won the Japan Cup! I was out getting hammered every night we were away. We all went our separate ways at first, then would be walking back to the hotel, seeing lads in the bars and joining up. The sing-songs began and there were some brilliant ones. The late-lamented Steve Carney played the piano, Waddle fancied himself on the spoons and we had a lot of bottle tappers!

Keegan would make one beer last the night while Arthur was a strict disciplinarian who only drank in moderation. We played at Kuala Lumpur first before flying on to Bangkok. When we got to our hotel in Thailand it was full of prostitutes. There were square landings on each floor and you could look right down to the entrance area. On every floor there were two or three prostitutes walking round knocking on doors. Suddenly there was a big kerfuffle down below as Arthur complained bitterly, saying he would refuse to play the game the next day unless there was a change of hotel.

We settled into another place, on the way towards the airport. It was lovely. In the evenings, we would have a meal followed by drinks. Stan Seymour, the Chairman, was a larger-than-life character who loved a drink and a smoke and he got in amongst us each night. Sometimes I had to put him to bed which was a feat in itself. Stan must have been twenty-odd stone and virtually impossible to get into the lift. When we finally reached his room he would whisper,

'See that case over there, SOSS? There's a bottle of whisky in it. Open it and pour us one, mate. Have one with me.' It was never just one!

We were sitting in a hotel in Bangkok one night. I'd had three or four Irish coffees, so had Coxy which was rare for him. Suddenly there was this commotion and Chris Waddle, Steve Carney and Kenny Wharton are being chased through the hotel by a Thai rickshaw driver! They had been messing around in the back of his vehicle and one of them had toppled over and accidentally put his foot through the canvas roof! Arthur asked me to find out what was happening and in the end they had a whip round for the driver.

One time we had been out all night and ordered a curry about five in the morning. Willie McFaul and I shared a room. We left the door open. When the young waiter delivered the order, I would deliberately jump into Willie's bed where he would be lying half-asleep.

'Get off me, you silly bugger!' he said. The lad steered the trolley into the wall as he watched with his mouth wide open!

'Just leave it over there, thanks,' I said, 'We'll get it when we're ready!'

By the pool with Willie McFaul

We took the bullet train to Nagoya and while we were there a lot of the lads went on a trip to Hiroshima, the first city in history to be targeted by a nuclear weapon back in 1945. I didn't join them. When the lads returned I could tell by what they were saying that some of them were really moved by the experience. It made me wish that I had gone with them. After all, I would probably never get a chance again. My trouble was that I took in too much nightlife and often missed opportunities to see things along the way. I made a bit more of an effort after that.

After the Thailand trip, Arthur asked me if I could go with the youth team to Amsterdam.

'Just make sure you turn up for the two games we've organised, otherwise your time's your own. It's a little bit of a reward and thanks for all your hard work so enjoy it.'

That was quite a gesture for someone like me. I went with Colin Suggett and the club secretary, Russell Cushing. Russell carried all the money because he paid the bills. He used to say to me and Willie McFaul on away trips, 'Make sure you stay close'.

After a night out in Amsterdam I got back to the hotel. I opened the door and my room was totally empty. All the furniture had disappeared so had my belongings! I went looking, walked round the corner and they'd set it up in the corridor! It was Gazza and his mates behind the prank. I'd had a skin full over the last few hours so I thought,

'Fuck it. I'm going to pitch down here.'

I went to sleep in my 'room' in the corridor! Come the morning, people were trying to get past while I'm in bed and I'm looking up and saying, 'Morning.' The lads came round the corner and pissed themselves. They thought that the fact that it hadn't bothered me was hilarious.

Russell and I sampled the nightlife in Amsterdam while Colin stayed back at base. We must have been away for five or six days in all. I'm sure that if Colin met me now he'd say to me, 'I'm surprised you're still alive'. I burnt the candles at both ends but I had a load of fun.

Another Newcastle trip was to Hamburg. All the action was in the Reeperbahn, a street which is at the centre of the night-life and in the red-light district. We were on a pre-season trip to play Hamburg so the players couldn't go out but we did! It was the first time I'd seen a live sex show and it wasn't really my scene. They were so far away on the stage you could barely see what they were up to. One of my patients went to Hamburg recently and asked me to recommend some parts to go to. I said, 'Try the Reeperbahn.' He came back saying that it was worse than Amsterdam!

I had many roles at Newcastle. Some were on my job description, many weren't. I seemed to spend much of my time as an amateur psychologist dealing with player issues. It was a job which kick-started my career and I will always be grateful to Arthur Cox for appointing me. I was at a high-profile, successful club surrounded by fabulous players, many of whom became good friends. In amongst all the household names, one of my best pals was a lad called John Anderson, an Irish right back who started the same day as me. John signed on a free transfer from Preston North End but it was pretty low key because of the Keegan coup. He was tough, strong and hard without being dirty and only missed one league game in the promotion-winning season. He never flinched and when he got injured he always defied the odds and came back quicker than expected.

Treating my good mate John Anderson

John was a smashing lad. We teamed up and went out regularly with our wives. The two of us got into quite a few scrapes and unfortunately lost touch. I think John's in local radio in the north-east now. Joy kept in touch with his wife for a while but I remarried, as did John, and our lives separated.

Despite the success achieved on the pitch, there were major changes. Keegan had retired and Arthur left for Derby County. He had fallen out with the club about budgets and took a job with a club who had just been relegated to the Third Division. I wasn't surprised when he turned round the Rams fortunes. By 1987 they won the Second Division title to end a seven-year exile from the First Division. Jack Charlton replaced him at St. James' Park but did not last long. His was a more direct style, the fans didn't approve, pressure mounted and Big Jack walked out after limited success.

I remember when one or two of the lads were coming back voluntarily for training before Jack started. Willie McFaul and I supervised them. It was blowing a gale one day and we went into the gym for a five-a-side. In walked Charlton, half-mast cords, scruffy shoes and check shirt. He called everyone together,

'You can forget about this. You'll be playing one-twos with him up there.'

Like fools everyone looked up to the rafters. Charlton added, 'With God.' He then told us all to go outside and stand forty yards apart in pairs.

'You're going to kick the ball as high as you can, one ball between two.' Waddle was running round like a little schoolboy. As for Terry McDermott, it was a case of, 'You can fuck off,' and he walked away. Later he had a meeting with Charlton, who said,

'I'm not sure about you. I want to see you play before I make my mind up.'

'You've been watching me for the last fifteen bloody years,' said Terry. And off he went. I, too, was to walk away from the north-east.

Chapter Eight

BACK TO MANCHESTER

'Bloody hell, I'm better than some of these players!'

I had seen a job at Oldham Athletic advertised in the Daily Mail and was immediately interested in the chance to get back home to Manchester. I applied and went down for an interview in the board room at Boundary Park. It must have been May or June 1984. I was met by Oldham manager Joe Royle, Chairman Ian Stott and a couple of directors. Like Newcastle, Oldham had been in the old Second Division but the two clubs had had conflicting fortunes in the 1983-84 season. Whereas Newcastle had just gained promotion Oldham had finished the season just one place above the drop zone although, to be fair, there was a five-point gap over Derby County below them.

The advert was appealing and suited my needs exactly. Apart from the obvious attraction of the Manchester area it required a first-team physiotherapist to open a private clinic at the ground. I had given two good years to Newcastle and enjoyed every minute but it was within narrow guidelines, dealing with footballers and football injuries. My aim coming out of college was always to work for a local football team and have my own practice. I had decided that there was a niche in the market for someone who specialised in injuries to the amateur sports player, the type who does it for fun at the grass roots level. At Tranmere we were negotiating for me to get £60 per week and to treat outsiders at the ground. It meant they could get me on the cheap. Oldham, however, wanted to make money out of it.

When I bumped into Joe Royle he immediately recognised me from his Everton days. This was flattering as when we last met he was in the first team at nineteen while I was the sixteen-year old, fresh-faced youth striving to justify a contract. Joe's initial words put me at ease as I waited for the interview:

'Oh, it's you! Are you still playing?'

'When Arthur Cox lets me!'

'You'll be alright here, then, we even had to get the lad out of the office to turn out last season!'

That little snippet of conversation set the tone for what was to be a brilliant chapter in my life. What Joe said did eventually happen to me. I was to come off the Oldham bench in my first game for the reserves in the Central League and score against Wolves . . . and it was with my first touch of the ball!

Cutting courtesy of the 'Oldham Evening Chronicle'

My fortunes quickly dipped as I dislocated an elbow in a charity soccer match a few days later and missed the trip to Blackpool with the second-team.

Despite him recognising me, I didn't know Joe other than our brief contact at Everton. It was the start of a wonderful relationship with the big man who had turned to management a couple of years earlier in the summer of 1982 after a fantastic club career, particularly at Everton between 1966 and 1974. He made his first team debut at sixteen, replacing Alex Young who was a fans idol at Goodison Park. He proved himself to the Blues fans with 102 league goals and was their leading scorer for five seasons. As well as a football legend, Joe was also a very intelligent man. He used to run businesses in his playing days. He bought and sold cars and ran a Littlewoods seconds outlet. He would definitely have made a success of his life outside football had he chosen to go down that route.

So, the prospects at Oldham were good. I got the job and was back on home ground doing all the elements of my work that I liked and on decent pay. I had been on around £150 per week at Newcastle and the figure was similar at Oldham. The club were certainly intent on making me work for my wage packet. I had to cover first team, reserve and youth games. However, doing youth games on a Saturday was not usually possible because of the clash with a first team game. I was also the kit man. If one of the coaches didn't turn up I willingly took some coaching sessions. On top of all that, I had to join in practice games because there were not enough numbers. The whole package was physically demanding but I quickly loved every minute because I felt such an important part of the set up.

Being back in the Manchester area was brilliant. We moved to Ashton-on-Mersey and Joy got a job at a school in Wythenshawe teaching Art. In the early days I used to go round to Joe's house for tea. We became very good friends. He has a smashing family. We are still in touch and I have many fond memories of them.

One of my first thoughts about Oldham Athletic was looking at the lads playing in the early games of the 1984-85 season and thinking, 'Bloody hell, I'm better than some of these players!' And they had been in the same league as Newcastle last year!

Oldham has had its fair share of troubles in a history going back to 1895. It soon became apparent to me that to survive as a Division Two side we had to beg, steal and borrow. Behind the scenes minor miracles were being performed year in, year out to keep the side afloat.

Joe often told me about what he had needed to do when he arrived as manager two years earlier. Things were so tight that he would regularly look for players in local Sunday League games,

'We only had 16 or 17 players and during my first year as manager and coach, I even bought towels for training. I didn't realise at the time they had semi-naked women on them, but they were catalogue surplus, hard-wearing and saw us through the season. We didn't have any weights so I bought some from a friend who was changing the equipment at his gym. They were the most antiquated weights you will ever see but we didn't have any so they were welcome. I cleaned the dressing room floor, scrubbed the treatment room . . . and even marked the numbers of the shirts and still have the stencil kit.'

Extract taken from 'Pinch Me Not' by Tony Bugby.

I learned that he had a visit from the bailiffs on his first day of training and he would be out most nights raising the profile of the club in pubs and clubs.

We relied on the absolute minimum staffing-wise. Apart from Joe, three of us did everything. I worked with assistant manager Billy Urmson and coach Willie Donachie. We did it all between us. They've probably got more staff hired as just fitness coaches these days at Manchester City.

Billy and I looked after the kit. Billy was Oldham through and through. He served the Latics for twenty-seven years and will be mainly remembered as youth team coach. Joe described him as the 'best in the business' and Billy reckoned that he produced at least thirty trainees who went on to make a living from the game. We couldn't compete with the big clubs for getting the pick of the crop. We often had to settle for second best but Billy did a great job transforming them. Mike Milligan and Nick Henry were two examples who owe him a debt, another was Paul Gerrard. They made themselves into top players after Billy had given them the foundations. Enthusiastic and honest all the time, Billy was great company and I loved working with him.

Willie Donachie and I started at the same time. Willie had forged a successful playing career by then, playing over 350 games at left-back for Manchester City and 35 times for Scotland. He came to Oldham as a player but also to work under Joe as a coach. Willie made 169 appearances over a six-year period but also played a huge part in his coaching capacity. He was incredibly fit, a model professional in every way. This athleticism kept him going as a player until he was 40 while he was still turning out for the reserves at 42.

Willie was a man of few words, the quiet, shy bloke who complimented Joe's high-profile. Joe would turn and ask him,

'Got anything to say, Willie?'

The answer came back, 'Yeah. That was shit.'

The two seemed to be joined at the hip. Willie's attention to detail in training was exceptional and, despite being untried in management, he and Joe formed a really good partnership. Joe was the front man who handled the press, something Willie wasn't comfortable with. He just wanted to coach. The two of them got hold of discarded players and moulded them. Willy worked on putting mistakes right. If you couldn't improve the players you had, you moved them on for others.

Despite not saying two words when one would do Willie Donachie was light years ahead of other coaches in his thinking. His approach is now more the norm but back in the mid-80's he was a ground-breaker and used the expertise that could come from fitness and sprint coaches among others. He had been one of Malcolm Allison's players at Manchester City and that had given him access to another coach who was innovative and forward-thinking. Allison employed sports psychologists, as did Willie. For an unfashionable club we were ahead of our time in that respect.

I remember the aerobics sessions with Joyce Kelsall, the club doctor's wife. Players used to be clambering over each other to get to the front row! To be fair, Joyce was a bit of a looker but took all the banter in good humour as she was experienced at taking groups. Husband, John, was a smashing fella and used to take a lot of ribbing from the lads about the missus! He took it all in his stride. I stood at the back of the classes and it was hilarious watching their uncoordinated bodies. Striker, Roger Palmer, would be all over the place while keeper Paul Gerrard would go left when the rest went right. We would bring Joyce in for a short burst of four or five sessions then move on to something else, much to the disappointment of the lads!

A local athletics coach came in for sprinting drills and we also employed Lennie Heppell, a dance teacher and father-in-law of former Newcastle player, Pop Robson. Lennie was another tutor way ahead of his time as an expert on dance and rhythm and used to take the top ladies tennis players to help get them around the court more easily. He also specialised in helping footballers and advised greats such as Bobby Moore, Peter Shilton and Alan Ball. At Boundary Park he had the Oldham lads doing dance steps and such-like while certain more sluggish players could expect an invitation to his house for a couple of days where they would be encouraged to move around quickly without lounging around. Lennie would even hide the remote on the telly so that they had to get up to change the programme. It was all about livening themselves up and having a brighter approach to life.

Willie studied every aspect of the game. He was the ideal man to think through how Oldham Athletic could benefit from having an artificial playing surface. I was a couple of years into my time at Oldham when the club took the decision to install a synthetic surface. For a club operating at a loss year-on-year this was a potential money-making venture as revenue could potentially be generated 365 days a year from use by the local community and beyond. There were other examples at QPR, Preston and Luton Town. Ultimately, they were banned but not before ours had shown me first-hand that it could improve players' techniques. It marked an upturn in the club's fortunes which I don't see as just a co-incidence.

Depending on what we were due to play on at the weekend, we would train on the same surface during the week. If we were away and on grass we would practice slide tackling, for instance, because that was one thing that you just didn't do on plastic. Plastic taught defenders to stand up more. Willie worked on passing and if you were a few centimetres out the ball would fly off and gather pace. He used to practice drills on the pitch time after time and it improved our passing game no end. You took it away with you on to grass and reaped the benefits.

The surface gave us a massive advantage because teams were psychologically 1-0 down before they had kicked off. It wasn't like the more advanced pitches of today, rather a layer of carpet on concrete. The ball often bounced twenty feet in the air! On top of that, Boundary Park was the country's second highest ground and the wind howled around the stands making it even trickier to deal with. It suited Oldham's style of play which gave us even more of a help. We played to feet, used two wingers and had our game-plan crafted by the master tactician in Willie Donachie.

We always had plenty of pace from the back and could take liberties on the plastic, sometimes playing with just two defenders because we knew that if the ball bounced over the lads it was the keeper's every time. The one at QPR had even more bounce than ours. The keeper would kick the ball upfield and one bounce took it over our crossbar!

The plastic pitch was a bonus in winter when other games were being called off. You could use it as a training facility without annoying the groundsman. Previously we had sat around waiting for someone to find somewhere to play. The only weather problem we had to contend with now was when it was blowing a gale because the ball went all over the place. You still got injuries but the plastic pitch took a lot of bodily contact out. Long term, however, I'm guessing that certain players suffered in later years with knee, ankle, hip and back injuries from an unforgiving surface.

Beyond the plastic pitch we trained at Little Wembley, a small area behind Boundary Park. Someone had given it that nickname before I had arrived. It certainly bore no resemblance to the national stadium! It was awful! The surface was full of holes which appeared like exploding mines and if it rained the area quickly became like a bog. It became unplayable in the winter. I know that Joe used to go past regularly on a Sunday and have to stop to chase off kids who had squeezed through the bars to play on it. Before the plastic arrived, he would shout, 'Get off our training pitch, it's all we've got!'

Before the arrival of the plastic pitch, the state of Little Wembley meant that we had to constantly find alternatives in inclement weather. We used the British Aerospace ground at the Lancaster Club and would often ring local schools to use their pitches. I quickly got used to doing deals. I 'borrowed' gyms for the injured lads to work in. There was one at the top of the road called Al'z Gym. It was one of the floors in an old mill. We ran the lads round in the afternoons, up the stone steps and on to the floor for a circuit. Al was a great lad, just starting up at the time. We repaid him with match tickets. His gym wasn't an elaborate place, more for body-builders and they laughed at our puny lads as they tried to lift the smaller weights. I met the lads twice a week at Royton Baths, from eight till nine in the morning. We jumped in with the public and did twenty lengths before returning to the ground. On the way we'd stop for a loaf of bread and the girls at the ground made us tea and toast.

We occasionally organised sessions at Oldham Leisure Centre for the whole squad. Remember, this was before the modern gyms like DW had opened. It was a bit easier to do deals in those days. Now they are looking for you to pay a corporate membership before using any of the facilities. There were bargaining tools in those days, though. Match tickets was an obvious one and we could also offer advertising space in programmes and around the ground. Joe and a couple of directors bought their own gym at nearby Shaw. It was a bit more than an ordinary gym but we used it for five-a-side.

Chapter Nine

PULLING RABBITS FROM THE HAT

'Denis could play with a pair of carpet slippers on'

Success at Oldham was measured by staying in the league and perhaps having the bonus of a little cup run. There was a standing joke around Boundary Park, however, that the club went on cup walks rather than cup runs! The players and staff would sit round the radio each year hoping for a big club away in the FA Cup but frequently ended up with a trip to a Hartlepool or a Torquay.

How Joe kept Oldham in the Second Division through the 1980's is unfathomable. I would frequently go into his office and say,

'I can't see us winning another game this season, boss.'

Joe would reply, 'Neither can I!'

But we always got through. This was very much his team by now. It was not full of household names but evolving all the time. As each season passed, Joe was showing how shrewd he was in the transfer market. With limited resources and an unfashionable name, it took an astute manager to make it work. Joe was learning fast. He had a good football brain and wasn't frightened of making tough decisions. One was to get rid of chief scout, Colin McDonald, and bring in Jim Cassell. Jim developed a successful scouting and youth policy before moving to Manchester City to oversee the development of their academy.

I used to say that to stay up Joe would have to pull a 'rabbit' out of the hat each season. One of the first was Mick McGuire. Mick was nearly 33 when he moved from Barnsley in 1985. He'd played the majority of his career at Norwich City. He wasn't the greatest of runners. If we did a lap of the pitch he would be half a lap behind. However, he could certainly play. Joe needed someone to get his foot on the ball in midfield and pass it and Mick was his man. He just sat in and started spreading the ball around. We had young up and coming hopefuls such as Mike Milligan and Nick Henry and Mick taught them a lot. Milligan and Henry came to be known as the 'Yard Dogs' in central midfield, snapping away at players. Jimmy Frizzell christened the name after we'd beaten his Manchester City side. We made light of it to the extent that Gordon, the Commercial Manager, went out and bought three thousand blow-up dogs for the fans. We'd be going to a game for a while after and see grown-up men carrying full size blow up dogs under their arms! That sort of touch was typical of the club at the time.

Milligan and Henry were dynamite together and could play a bit as well. They kept the ball moving round the park. The club had released Nick to Norway on loan and he came back a different player. Milligan came in on a government scheme. Jim Cassell identified 'this kid in Manchester' who had potential and we trusted his judgement. Mike made his debut against Liverpool in a pre-season friendly and got himself into such a tangle with nerves that he was ill after the game. Over the years he grew with us and grew as a man. He wasn't always the captain but was always a leader. You knew what you got with the likes of Milly.

Another 'rabbit' out of the hat at around the same time was Paul Jones, once described as the best uncapped centre-half of his generation. I knew Paul from Ellesmere Port days. He went on to spend most of his career at Bolton Wanderers and was a player there for thirteen years, clocking up well over 400 games. We were having a bit of a crisis, and two injuries was a crisis for a small squad like ours, when Joe said to me one day,

'I've got a friend of yours signing.'

He told me who and straight away I thought it would be a good move for the club. Joe had gone to watch Huddersfield and Jonesy had played even though he hadn't been in their side for a while with injuries. Their manager, Mick Buxton, was unwilling to let him out on a free but came back to Joe and said,

'Give us ten grand, Joe.'

Jonesy was the wrong side of thirty by then. He came in to sign the deal at Christmas and had just been to Huddersfield's Christmas party. He breathed on the Chairman who then pulled Joe to one side,

'Are we doing the right thing here?'

Joe said, 'Chairman, he's just a popular boy.' He'd been on several club parties and was about to go on ours! He didn't ask anything about the contract, just,

'When's your Christmas do?'

'Tonight.'

'Right, count me in.'

He never went back home for three nights. When Jonesy left Joe's office to sign the forms, I swear Joe looked at me and started laughing!

'He'll do for us, won't he, SOSS?'

What Joe saw was a man who embodied the Oldham spirit and, sure enough, Paul Jones was to get the changing room going as well as show how good a player he was. We had to look after him though. Sometimes he'd come in and Joe would look at him and say,

'Knee a bit sore, Jonesy? Go and make the toast. Do a few exercises with SOSS. Hang around with him for a while.'

Paul should have had fifty caps. The game was so easy for him. I played with him for Cheshire Schoolboys and as a young player he looked like a Rolls Royce. When Oldham signed him the Roller was a bit aged with a loose exhaust but he had an influence, not least on Andy Linighan. Paul definitely improved Andy as a player. He would constantly marshall Andy, always repeating the order,

'Whatever you do make sure you are never behind me.'

We were defending on the half way line against Bradford City. Joe called it condensing the pitch. It was the most blatant offside trap you'd ever see and Jonesy must have caught Don Goodman fifteen or twenty times. We called him the 'Step-up King'. Goodman later complained in the paper about Oldham's negative tactics. Joe said,

'Negative tactics? What's he on about? He's so thick he just kept running offside. That's not negative.'

As with Mick McGuire, Paul stayed about three years but both left having done the job that Joe had asked of them and brought that little bit of experience, quality and steel to our team. Jonesy could run a back four and did a wonderful job.

Then there was John Kelly. What a character he was! John came 'out of the hat' in 1987, a midfielder who was struggling to establish himself with Swindon Town after around three hundred games for his home team Tranmere Rovers, Preston North End and Chester City. We were coming back from Swindon after getting battered and on the coach we were watching the film 'Critters'. It's about a bunch of small, furry aliens who make lunch out of humans. Joe and I turned to each other and said,

'That's what we need in midfield.'

We had been over-run by Lou Macari's direct, energetic Swindon side and we'd been trying to play nice football. We needed more energy in the middle of the park. During the game I kept seeing John Kelly warming up. I'd known him since my days in Liverpool. John also had a habit of leaning into the dug-out and smiling at us! Very strange! Well, Joe and I decided that we needed some Critters. We thought of Kel and said, 'There's one. He even looks like one!' We signed him for thirty thousand. Lou said he wasn't keen on him anyway because he liked the drink too much. To be fair to John, there was no one fitter.

John was not the best of players but would run all day and loved a party. He was larger than life and played his part in getting us a few results which helped us stay in the league. Eventually the younger ones would come through but John had done his job. Joe recognised how important it was to get personalities in as well as footballers and players such as John Kelly were to fit the bill perfectly.

Joe constantly watched reserve team football in Central League games and built up a portfolio of players he might be interested in. With Jim Cassell he would be out perhaps four times a week. One particular target was the reserve teams at big clubs such as Everton, Leeds and Manchester City. When Joe was offered the Manchester City job, Chairman Peter Swales asked him if there were any players in the youth team who were likely to make it. It was a strange question to ask a man thinking of coming in to the club but Joe was out so often watching reserves and youth games that he probably knew the team better than some already inside the club.

Joe returned to the scene of former glories and brought Neil Adams and Ian Marshall from Everton. Earl Barrett and Paul Warhurst came from Manchester City as did Paul Moulden and Ian Thompstone. Ian's stay was sadly affected by injury but Joe had done his homework to get these type of players, moulded them into his team and eventually they moved on better and stronger. There was some amazing business done when you consider the transfer fees that some of them eventually commanded.

This approach for players just wouldn't be possible today. The market's changed so much. Back then Joe could offer City reserve team players five or ten pounds a week more to come to Oldham and they'd bite his hand off. Today there are unknowns in the reserves at the Etihad who will be on a few grand a week!

One of many gems unearthed was Earl Barrett. A search for regular first-team football brought Earl to Boundary Park in 1987 and he was a wonderful player with an engaging smile which always lit up the place. Joe told the Chairman that the club would make money on him and they sure did. He came for thirty grand and left for £1.7 million! As I remember, Joe started him at left back and Earl's started slide tackling on the plastic pitch! Fans soon gave him the nickname 'Psycho'. As a defender and athlete Earl was second to none. He was thin around the waist yet built like a light heavyweight in the top half. He had an amazing leap which often took him above much taller players and he could get all over players like a rash. Earl was also called 'The Rucksack' because he would stick to the back of forwards. He could read a game brilliantly although distribution occasionally let him down. Joe used to joke that Earl was best at centre-half because he could slice it either way and still keep it on the pitch! England caps were achieved but sadly Earl retired with knee problems after spending time at Everton and Aston Villa.

Earl formed a fantastic centre-back partnership with Richard Jobson. Joe broke the club's transfer record for the third time in a month when he took Jobbo from his home-town team, Hull City, in 1990. His move came as a result of a knee ligament injury to Andy Holden in a midweek game against Leicester City. Andy was one mean centre half. He had a habit of butting the back of people's heads if he lost the first header. He was so ferocious he often injured himself in the process. I had to take him off time after time for stitches. The £460 000 fee for Richard Jobson beat the money paid out for John Keeley, from Brighton, and David Currie, from Nottingham Forest. 'Jobbo' became a Boundary Park favourite, playing nearly two hundred games over the next five seasons.

I reckon that if you threw a brick into the penalty area Jobbo would have headed it out first and asked questions later. Despite getting knocked round a bit, particularly to his face, he never shirked a challenge. He was a gentle man off the pitch but learned to mix it with some of the game's most physical attackers, the likes of Ian Wright and John Fashanu. I don't think that Jobbo had a fight in him but when it came to winning the ball from physical opponents he did it with great regularity.

Fashanu was one big unit, a constant physical presence and a black belt in karate. He used his elbows a lot in the days when they weren't pulled up for it. Centre forwards of stature would hit the centre halves back when clattered. No stature and they would go away and hide somewhere.

We were at Selhurst Park when Wimbledon played there and there had been a real tussle going on. Just before half time Fashanu laid Jobbo out after Richard was gaining the upper hand. Fashanu waited for his moment. He watched the ball come over, knew exactly where Jobbo was and lamped him. Fashanu knew it was on purpose as did the Wimbledon bench. Jobbo went down dazed but I managed to bring him round and we got him into the changing room. His head was all over the place. I told them to block the dressing room door. The doctor was trying to get in and I wanted to keep him out because I knew that if he examined Jobbo he would stop him going back out again. The lad was definitely groggy and we had to let the doctor see him in the end but if it had been an immediate check there would have been no chance of him going back out. This was in the days of discretionary risks. Nowadays the player simply wouldn't be allowed back out.

The lads, including Jobbo, had gone back out for the second half. I was collecting medical gear ready to follow. Joe and I would usually walk out together. Anyway, the door opened and in came Fashanu, dressed in flip-flops and towel. It was obvious that he had been substituted. He started having a go at Joe for influencing Joe Kinnear into taking him off.

'I thought you were better than that, Joe,' he said.

Joe replied, 'John, you were out of order, mate.'

'Come on, Joe, you must have done something like that in your career.'

'No, I was better than that, John. Remember, I could play.'

There was no coming back from that put down. Joe simply brushed John out of his way and left the changing room. I didn't know then that Joe and John went back a way because when Joe was at Norwich City at the end of his playing career, John and his brother Justin used to stay with him. They had a difficult upbringing following the splitting up of their parents and Joe did his bit to help. Jobbo, incidentally, went back out and didn't shirk one header.

Joe went to watch Paul Warhurst play for City reserves. The lad was elegant but just lacking real desire. When he never came out in the second half Joe spoke to Mel Machin about it,

'What happened to him, Mel?'

'Oh, he's going to Chesterfield tomorrow on a free or something.'

Well, he was better than any of our reserves and we were having another of our famous crises. Joe said to Mel,

'Tell you what. He might as well come to us as go there.'

That was a big statement from an Oldham manager because Joe used to joke that we had to have two board meetings to make a decision about a free transfer. The clubs spent a couple of days haggling. Because Earl Barrett had done so well for thirty thousand, Mel came back and said,

'Look, Joe, sorry about this, it's embarrassing but we can only let Paul go if you pay us ten grand. The board say we cannot give another one away.'

Paul went straight into the side at Portsmouth in 1988. Just before we went out he gave me his inhaler to look after and that was the first time I realised that he had asthma. We didn't do medicals in the same way in those days. There came a point when Paul needed it. Imagine looking across from Joe's position. With ten minutes to go he sees me throw something to Paul from out of my bag.

'What the hell is that, SOSS?'

'Inhaler, boss.'

'He's asthmatic? They hid that from us! I thought it was a grenade!'

The colder air at Oldham seemed to affect Paul more. He was very quick but only in bursts. The club doctor and I decided to send him to a chest specialist in Manchester who changed his medication and changed his career.

The next problem was a hernia. We got it sorted out over the summer and Paul was soon back doing pre-season over the road at the Blue Bell pitches behind the squash club. Joe comes across and watches the lads running when he notices this player cruising round the pitch. It was Paul Warhurst, asthma and hernia sorted. He quickly showed that he was different class. He grew with the club and we sold him for £800k. At Manchester City they had called him 'Barrett's revenge' after Earl's success had persuaded Oldham to part with some cash but in the end it turned out to be 'Royle's revenge.' Big Joe had pulled off another coup.

Paul is the quickest player with a ball at his feet that I have seen. In fact, he could run as fast with the ball as without it. He could sprint from defence and be at the opponent's area in a matter of three or four seconds. A lot of players run fast but slow down when they kick the ball. Not Paul Warhurst. He was so smooth and versatile. This speed caught many other teams by surprise.

One question mark against him was his toughness. Graeme Sharp had laid him out in an FA Cup tie which went to three replays before we ended up winning. I got on to the pitch and found Paul in tears. Sharpy had really hurt him. Earl Barrett and I told him to get up. Earl urged him to not let Sharp know that he'd hurt him otherwise he was done for. You didn't have to take them off to come back on in those days. Kevin Sheedy took the ball immediately, looked up and floated a ball across to Sharp. Warhurst was nowhere and Sharp scored. We got a draw that day and took them back to Boundary Park. I'm not implying that Paul was soft. It's just that because of that kind of thing he wasn't a natural centre half. Joe fancied him at full-back and he went to Sheffield Wednesday for £750 000 where he played as a defender but injuries to David Hirst and Mark Bright saw him used as an emergency striker. He scored twelve goals in as many games and was called up as a striker for England! He was to play as defender and, occasionally, forward at Blackburn before a spell at Bolton in midfield!

Elland Road was a particularly fruitful place to plunder. Leeds had a fantastic youth system which yielded players of the quality of Denis Irwin, Andy Ritchie, Andy Linighan and Tommy Wright. We reckoned that manager, Billy Bremner, was our best scout at the time! Andy Linighan came for £55000 and was a brilliant investment while a director paid for Wright in 1986 and took his money back and more when Oldham sold him to Leicester City three years later. We also had enough left in the kitty to buy Rick Holden from Watford. Leeds eventually got to the stage where they had had enough and said that Joe couldn't have any more!

Denis Irwin was typical of a player who was transformed under the Royle-Donachie regime. The Irish-born full-back began his career with Leeds United in 1983, making seventy-two appearances for the Yorkshire side before being given a free transfer in 1986. Shattered and disillusioned, he went home to Cork and drank it dry! Who would have thought that he would emerge from the bars near his home to play at the very highest level for Manchester United and the Republic of Ireland. He has Joe Royle to thank for that. Joe signed Denis after advice from Jim Cassell and his scouting team. Despite being given a free transfer, Joe saw an exceptional talent and the deal was completed in May 1986 which was unusual for us because normally we wouldn't want to pay a player through the summer before he had even kicked a ball. However, Joe and Chairman Ian Stott were so worried about losing him to another club that they felt it had to be done. Joe had assured the Chairman that the club could make a lot of money from this lad. Ian replied,

'Well, we'd better go and get him then.'

Oldham Athletic squad 1986-87. Picture courtesy of the 'Oldham Evening Chronicle'

Back (left): *Denis Irwin, Paul Jones, Andy Goram, Andy Gorton, Andy Linighan, Roger Palmer* **Middle:** *Willie Donachie (player-coach), Andy Barlow, Ron Futcher, Darron McDonough, Me, John Ryan, Tony Henry, Mick McGuire, Billy Urmson (coach)* **Front:** *Gary Williams, Bob Colville, Paul Atkinson, Joe Royle (manager), Mike Cecere, Mike Milligan, Gary Hoolickin.*

Denis was good enough to play at right-back or left but could read the game so well that he was also effective from centre half. I always reckoned that he could play with a pair of carpet slippers on and a cigar in his mouth. It was that easy for him. Denis was quick and he had two very good feet.

On the first day of pre-season, just after Denis signed, we had a jog-walk from the ground up to a local monument in Tandle Hill Park. You can see the monument from the M62 when you come off at Junction 20. The run was a traditional start of season test for a group of lads who had done nothing since April. In those days there was no fitness regime to pursue during the summer and this was a killer for some of them!

It was an easy pace under Billy Urmson. Well, we got to the top and Denis wasn't with us. Joe wondered where he could be and asked me to go and look for him because he was new to the area. I jogged back down and found him. He was really struggling for breath. It was an inauspicious start. Through careful nurturing, Joe transformed the fortunes of Denis Irwin. It is never easy when young impressionable lads are released by big clubs such as Leeds. They can easily fall by the way side and it could have gone either way for Denis but he was fortunate. Denis played 167 games in four years at Oldham. The free transfer then moved on to the biggest club in the land, signing at Old Trafford for a fee of £625 000. All in all, a good bit of business!

When Alex Ferguson was about to take him on he said,

'Joe, we've watched Denis about twenty times and every report's been good. Is he that good?' He said later that Denis was one of the best signings he'd ever made and he earned the name 'eight out of ten Denis' as a tribute to his consistency.

Playing alongside Denis Irwin in my all-time team would be Andy Goram. Andy was a young and up and coming goalkeeper but already established at Oldham when I arrived. The Bury-born lad could put his hand to anything. He was very good at cricket, golf and snooker. People said he was too small to be a goalkeeper. I believe he was half an inch short of six foot but he'll tell you he was six foot. As a keeper and shot stopper he was the best I have worked with. With one-on-one shot stopping Andy was second to none. You would put your money on him to save. He said that the trick was to stand and look them in the eye. All players have to look at the ball at the point they are going to strike. As soon as their head dropped, Andy pounced. He could make up to ten yards in the time it took the attacker to look down, lift the kicking leg back and bring it forward to the ball. One season he had a competition with the reserve keeper Andy Gorton. Gorton was potentially as good, replacing Goram for a while when he moved north, before being released. The pair would see how many players they could they get carried off in a season. It was quite a few!

Andy Goram was a naturally fit lad who loved to play out in training sessions in five-a-sides. He fancied himself as a striker and typical of such a talented guy he wasn't bad either. This country didn't see the best of him. Shortly after the incident on the coach which Joe talked about, Andy moved to Hibernian. He had been getting frustrated with life and there had been growing personal problems. He needed the move as much as we needed the cash. I read at the time that Hibs were going to sign Ian Andrews from Southampton for £150-200k. Joe rang Saints assistant manager Peter Cormack who was a big mate from Bristol City days.

'If you want a goalkeeper why not go for the best down here. He might cost you a bit more but he'll be worth it. If you want him for £300k he's yours and if you don't think he's worth it after a month we'll take him back.'

Andy was a terrific keeper. He was top notch. Peter rang a week later and said, 'We can't believe how good he is.' From there he went to Rangers for a million and was a massive player at Ibrox.

Paul Gerrard made his name as Oldham's keeper later in my time at Boundary Park. The apprentice was quite different from Andy Goram in that he was a man-made keeper. As a young lad at Oldham, Paul had legs like Bambi. There was no strength in them and his kicking was abysmal. I came across him a lot because of recurrent dislocations of his knee-cap. I used to regularly flick the kneecap back into place. He had operations on both knees to tie them in and then he worked so hard on strengthening his legs.

The back pass rule changed football, particularly for goalkeepers. Paul struggled to cope with this at first but practised and practised. After slashing at balls, keepers started to take a touch and play the ball out. Ultimately, he mastered it and became a tremendous keeper. One day he was having a bad time. We had been losing games and Paul was at fault with one or two of the goals we had been conceding. Joe brought Andy Dibble in on loan to put pressure on him. Now Dibbs was quite a character. I came across him later in my career at Accrington when he was goalkeeping coach. I don't think he'd mind me saying that he was a better coach than a goalkeeper. If a shot was off target Dibbs would save it, if it was on target he'd let it in.

Anyway, we were training on the pitch at Oldham. Dibbs was letting everything in. Joe turned to me and said, 'Do you think I've dropped a bollock here?' As luck would have it one of City's second or third-choice keepers got injured in training on the same day. City called Dibble back and Paul Gerrard went from strength to strength. He rose to the challenge and never looked back.

Chapter Ten

JOE

'Tell you what, let's try putting three passes together this half.'

Joe Royle worked tirelessly to create a side that competed week in, week out. Considering that this was his first job in management he learned so quickly and used his many qualities wisely. First and foremost he was brilliant with people. He would share a word or two with everyone at the club, from the cleaner upwards, in exactly the same way. He would always laugh and joke with them. Everyone would get Christmas presents from him.

Joe put his arm round players and got their confidence and self-belief going. At the same time, he didn't suffer fools. If you get one bad egg in a changing room it can spread like a cancer. I'm thinking of the sort of player who is unhappy and lets everyone else know about it. Joe didn't tolerate that.

We might go ten games without a win which would get you the sack now but we never ever felt threatened at Oldham. Nobody at the club thought for a moment that Joe would ever get the push. He had a fridge in his room, full of Budweiser and wine. Billy Urmson was often asked about Joe's best buy in his years at Boundary Park and his reply was, 'The fridge in his office!' I might come in feeling despondent about the number of injuries or lack of success and even at nine o'clock in the morning he'd tell me to put things into perspective and get a Bud out. I would leave his room fifteen minutes or so later with a smile on my face. Joe always reassured me that I was doing my best.

Contrasting emotions

We sometimes had a staff meeting where we went through every player in the club, helped by two or three beers. It was never enough beer to get us into a tangle . . . well, except for Billy who had the nickname Billy 'Two Lagers' Urmson. If he had the third it got messy! Our meetings were always kept informal, as was everything at Latics, and we would even have directors coming in and listening. Billy would make profound statements like, 'He's not good enough but I'll make him a player.' Joe would write down what Billy said, with date and time, and always reminded his mate if his words came back to haunt him further down the line!

Joe had a massive presence physically, 6'3" and broad, but was a gentle giant at heart. He was also fantastic with words. He didn't have to raise his voice. In his mind if you ranted and raved you had lost the plot. Constructive rather than destructive criticism was the order of the day. There were no temper tantrums like with some other bosses I've seen and worked with. In all the time I've known him I've only seen Joe have two stand-up rows, with Micky Quinn and Ian Marshall. They confronted him nose to nose. Micky Quinn had caught Joe's eye whilst scoring a bagful of goals at Stockport County and joined the club for £53000 in January 1984. He was to move on to Portsmouth a couple of years later for almost three times that amount. Anyone who has heard him on the radio will not be surprised when I say that Micky was a character and a half. He could hold his own and on one occasion prompted Joe to push him in the chest. Micky landed on his backside about ten yards away. There was one occasion at a Christmas do when one of the lads jumped on Micky's back and Micky slipped, tearing his hamstring. He was out for six weeks and we missed him because we relied on his goals at the time. Needless to say, Joe was not amused!

Ian Marshall made his name at Oldham as a striker after coming as a central defender from hometown club Everton in 1988. Marshy should have been an international. He was the fastest player in the side after twenty yards. Warhurst and Barrett were quicker over shorter distances but ten yards further and Marshy would have gone clear. He ate the ground up.

Ian scored forty goals in around 200 games but tried to ruin the after-match party for getting to the 1990 League Cup Final against Nottingham Forest. Ian had declared himself unfit before the game and overcame his disappointment by drinking himself into oblivion during it. Joe was not pleased.

Although reactions like that were rare from Joe he could be very cutting in a quieter way and his comments were often a source of amusement if they weren't aimed in your direction. Once we came in at half time and Joe said to the lads,

'Tell you what, let's try something different in the second half. Let's try putting three passes together.'

We had a goalkeeper called John Hallworth. John spent the majority of his career at Boundary Park and was the club's first-choice keeper for most of his time there, taking over from Andy Goram. I remember one particular game in which John was not being decisive in his decision-making. Joe let him know at the break,

'You're like Mavis Riley in goal. Should I, shouldn't I, should I? Just go for the bloody cross and stop dithering.'

Mavis was a character in Coronation Street who could never make her mind up. John's looking back at him, open-mouthed, and the rest are hiding their faces trying not to burst out laughing!

Then there was Joe McBride, a left winger we got from Everton via Rotherham United. Joe had drifted out of a game and was going into places we couldn't find him in. Players can sometimes hide in hard work, you know. Confidence might have gone or they could have the crowd on their backs. I have to say that Gazza was a notable exception. Whatever the occasion and the mood he was in, Gazza always wanted the ball and would be looking for it all the time. This wasn't the case with Joe McBride on this particular afternoon. Joe went up to him at half time and said,

'Joe, we can't find you with a bloody radar out there!' Again the changing room erupted but he had got his point across.

Gary Williams was a left-sided player, midfield or defence, and another who was the recipient of some of Joe's home-spun wit. Gary was so laid-back and Joe set about him at half-time.

'You're like Clive Dunn out there shuffling up and down the line.'

The former Dad's Army star had a big hit with a song called 'Grandad' in 1971. Anyway, the next game the lads brought in a flat cap and a pair of slippers and stuck them on Gary's peg! Whatever the other changes have been in my career, dressing room humour has always been there. It still happens. In any other walk of life you might class it as abuse, in football it is banter. If you're not a strong enough character it can overpower you. I ended up living with Gary Williams for a few months. I'd separated from my second wife and Gaz had a terraced house near Boundary Park. He invited me to stop in his spare room. Gaz and I used to be out every night. Tea would be five pints of Guinness. I went to Corfu at the end of the season. Back at Manchester Airport, I saw my wife. I said,

'What you doing here?'

She replied, 'I've come to take you home!'

In other words, you've been enjoying yourself too much. I went home meekly. Gary and I were good friends and he was my permanent patient with a knee injury. He eventually went back to Bristol, his birthplace, and has a couple of pubs, as did his father Alan, a former Oldham player.

Joe Royle's clever one-liners kept tripping off the tongue. He had a classic ahead of games at Old Trafford, saying to his coaching staff:

'We'll be lucky to get a corner today but don't tell the lads that.'

One year we all stood up and cheered when we got our first corner there. Everyone wondered what we were up to! So much went right for Joe but there were incidents from time to time which made it very clear how difficult a manager's life can be. Joe tells a story about when he was in bed one Christmas morning. Suddenly there was a phone call from one of the local Manchester gangsters who had somehow got his number. He told Joe that his keeper and a midfield player were going to have their kneecaps shot off.

'Why?' asked Joe.

'They filled my son in at a night club on Christmas Eve,' the reply came back.

One of our keepers ended up as an alcoholic. He was a good keeper, as well, and Joe tried his best to give him help but eventually let him go. He was off the drink when he returned but then went back on it. As a manager, Joe was dead against drink.

'You used to drink as a player,' I would say to him.

'Always at the right times, mate,' he would reply.

With much of Joe's period at Oldham Athletic spent helping to keep the wolf from the door it made it even more rewarding when some of the best times finally came along. Within a three-week period in April 1990, a classic FA Cup semi-final was followed by a first Wembley appearance in ninety-five years for the Littlewoods Cup. To keep a season going on three fronts was unknown at Boundary Park and some days we would get to the ground and see three queues for tickets, for the next League fixture, the FA Cup and the Littlewoods Cup. This was unprecedented for an unfashionable club and you must remember that back in those days the top teams didn't put out second strings for the cup games like they do today. It was also amazing to see these new highs after a season where we had finished a modest sixteenth in League Two, only seven points above relegation.

The epic season didn't start well, with two draws and two defeats, but a 3-2 home win over Plymouth Argyle got the ball rolling. Joe always reckoned that a win over Leeds United in the Second Round of the Littlewoods Cup was the catalyst. Any win against our old rivals was a good one. There was plenty of history between the clubs and not much distance between us across the Pennines on the map. Leeds had a new-look team after Howard Wilkinson had splashed the cash and to beat them home and away in the two-leg tie was a fantastic boost to the players and fans.

Frank Bunn then re-wrote the record books on a Wednesday night in October 1989, hitting six past Scarborough to take us to a Fourth Round tie against First Division champions Arsenal. The fans had seen nothing so far compared to what happened on that November night in Oldham. George Graham had got his side practising on a similar synthetic surface to ours and sent an awesome-looking line-up on to the pitch but the Yard Dogs were out at Boundary Park that night and we never gave them an inch. The lads hunted, snapped and infuriated the likes of Alan Smith and Niall Quinn and it was a magical night as we won 3-1 with two goals from Andy Ritchie and one from Nick Henry.

It was nose-bleed time as we reached the quarter finals to face Southampton. We were within seconds of going out of the competition but Andy Ritchie pounced again late in injury time to make the score 2-2 and take the tie back to Oldham. Southampton were unhappy about the amount of injury time and their mood wasn't helped by Joe jumping from the dug-out when we equalised and shouting at their bench, 'Plastic, back to plastic.' I know he wasn't too proud of that comment but in the heat of the moment . . . . It made a change because it was usually me saying the controversial things and getting into trouble.

Having got a bit of money from the cup run, we had hired a plane to take us to Southampton. This hadn't gone down well with Ian Marshall and Andy Ritchie who weren't keen on flying but it was all forgotten on the way back north! It was a mad, rocking Boundary Park night for the replay, a packed house and thousands locked out. They were unbelievable scenes. We were supposed to be an unfashionable club, weren't we?! Two nil. Ritchie and Milligan. Job done. Amazing.

Nobody could have predicted the first leg score line in the semi-final against West Ham United. 6-0? No way. It was 14th February 1990 and, of course, the press went to town with talk of a 'Valentine's Day Massacre.' Mike Milligan had appeared in the morning paper dressed in a gangster suit and holding a machine gun. That worried Joe because he didn't want it to have a positive effect on the Hammers.

Joe got it right tactically. Having seen a defensive-minded side against him he made a late decision to push Ian Marshall forward and it paid off. Three-up by half-time, we nailed a fantastic win. It made us red-hot favourites to get to Wembley but played with the minds of the lads and they were off the pace in the second leg, losing three nil which didn't please Joe. However, it was a wake-up call ahead of another important cup game just three days later in the FA Cup fifth round, against Joe's former club Everton.

Amidst the growing excitement surrounding the Littlewoods Cup run, we had made a low-key start in the FA Cup Third Round, just getting past Third Division Birmingham after a replay. The Fourth Round game at home to Brighton was just three days after the Southampton draw on the south coast in the Littlewoods. There was no doubt an effect on the lads but Joe changed Ian Marshall's role again, giving him the attacking duties that he loved and a three-pronged attack took us into the Fifth Round thanks to Scott McGarvey and Andy Ritchie's goals. The reward was a home tie against Everton.

An already congested fixture list was to get much busier as we arm-wrestled over three games. We finally got past Everton after extra-time thanks to a penalty from former-Blue Ian Marshall after 330 minutes of effort and toil which I'm convinced was to come back to haunt us later in the season. The drawn-out tie meant that we were to face Aston Villa in the quarter finals just four days later and only seven days after defeating West Ham to reach Wembley in the Littlewoods Cup. The fans were in dream land but the combined effort of three campaigns was bound to test even the strongest players as the games came thick and fast.

Many said that the bubble would burst and that we would get our come-uppance. Once again we proved the critics wrong. The First Division leaders came to Boundary Park and we beat them 3-0. Villa manager, Graham Taylor was very gracious, refusing to point to the plastic surface but praising our direct style of play. The massive prize was a semi-final against Manchester United at Manchester City's Maine Road ground.

It was a first semi-final for Oldham since 1913 and a brilliant occasion for the Greater Manchester area as well as one of those romantic ties that get the press and fans excited. The match was a classic, ending 3-3 after extra time. We could have won but Oldham's exploits were beamed around the world and had United manager Alex Ferguson describing us as the best side in Division Two. He and his side had got away with it and Alex knew that. However, it was a great statement from Oldham who showed that they could match the very best and on grass. The lads were a bit disappointed in referee Joe Worrall who called the United players by their Christian names and us by our surnames. Joe was a good official and probably didn't mean anything by it but it niggled all the same.

We took the lead after five minutes when Earl Barrett tapped in but Bryan Robson's goal took the teams into half-time level. Neil Webb gave the Reds the lead but we came back with an Ian Marshall volley. Extra-time was needed and United looked to have taken the tie again through Danny Wallace before Latics legend Roger Palmer popped up late to tie the game. Joe used to call Roger the 'Black Ghost'. He was such an elusive player who would just arrive in the right place and score goals, 156 of them for Oldham. It's a club record. One strange thing about Roger was that no one knew where he lived. He was picked up every day in Sale for eight years by Willie Donachie. Sometimes the weather would be foul but Roger still didn't want Willie to take him home or pick him up there. I took him a couple of times and dropped him off at a pub called 'The Piper'. It looked a bit rough and he invited me in for a drink. It reminded me of the pub in 'Shameless', the Channel 4 series on television. When I asked Roger where he lived he would point 'over there'. We knew that he was on the rougher side of Sale. Roger never drove, had no bank account. We had some real concerns about his lifestyle but let it go. After all, where were we going to get a 17 goal-a-season striker for nothing?

Three days later we squared up again on the same pitch and there was another exciting game for the fans. Joe was in the fantastic situation of having one Wembley trip in the bag and was desperate not to have another replay. I think it affected his thinking and we didn't set-up as defensively-minded as we might if we'd wanted to keep it tight, not be afraid of another replay and try to catch them on the break.

After Brian McClair had given United the lead, their former player Andy Ritchie stunned the Reds ten minutes from the end. It was extra time once again and Mark Robins scored a late winner, exploiting a big hole in our defence. As Andy Holden ran back after our equaliser he asked Joe what to do. Joe told him to stay up as he tried to avoid that extra replay. Robins ran through the middle where Andy would have been and United went on to beat Crystal Palace in the final. The game was controversial in that the TV replays showed that a Nick Henry effort in the first half had clearly crossed the line. I meet fans to this day who still complain that we were denied a second Wembley trip. However, one was more than we could have dreamed off at the start of the season and I was determined to savour every moment.

Chapter Eleven

WEMBLEY AND LIFE AT THE TOP TABLE

'It was a goal which changed many lives'

There's no doubt that the two ties against United had taken a lot out of the lads. Joe reckoned that we peaked in the 3-3 game and by the time the Littlewoods final arrived we were over the top. A number of players were either out injured or carrying niggles. Andy Holden lost his place after picking up a knock five days earlier at Portsmouth. We faced Brian Clough's Nottingham Forest in the final and all the games we had played disrupted our training. The sessions were more like warm-ups. A little bit of running, a lot of stretching and even more head tennis!

Going down Wembley Way that day was a memory that will stay with me forever and I was privileged to enjoy it again for an FA Cup semi-final four years later. You watch the day unfold on television every year from childhood and there's always a tear in the eye as the team coaches make their way slowly towards the ground with the adoring fans surrounding them. I made sure that I was right at the front of the coach, taking everything in.

A few of us were watching Forest warming-up when a couple of their back-room staff came out. Joe asked them if Cloughy was here yet. They replied, 'No'. Clough wasn't a nine-to-five man. He bucked the trends and was even known to occasionally give his players a week off!

Well, he eventually rolled up and appeared to have had a drink or two. I have to say that the Forest staff covered it really well. In the first half they put him on the second row of benches. He kept standing and shouting 'Jemson!' and each time he stood up, his staff did likewise so he wasn't isolated. I remember that he used to address players by their surnames.

Nick Henry passed a late fitness test but Ian Marshall had a thigh strain. We had surgeon Jonathan Noble down with us. I took Ian out from the hotel on the morning of the final for a fitness test and Jonathan came with us. Marshy could still feel it. Jonathan said that being a big game he could inject. For Marshy it was more a case of what happens after that.

'What if it tears?'

I told him, 'Then you miss the rest of the season but you might not get another Wembley appearance in your lifetime.'

Marshy couldn't cope. He could and should have played with an injection and got so frustrated with himself that he hadn't that he got into a bit of a tangle after the game. He stormed off to his room and proceeded to drink himself silly. It was a shame because he played a massive part in us getting there. It was our 61st game of the season and to make matters even more difficult it was a sweltering hot day. Joe reckoned that an accumulation of games proved to be our undoing and pointed to the fact that Des Walker, a Forest defender, was man of the match as testimony to the effort the lads put in. Our lads gave everything. I knew the likes of Milligan, Henry and Holden would go, go, go despite the hot conditions and the heavy schedule but we really missed Marshy's firepower. We were running on empty and both Irwin and Milligan were to have little operations afterwards.

Joe went for Frank Bunn in place of Marshall. Frank was in an even worse state with a bad knee after he'd been caught in a tackle at Leeds. Frank had more than his fair share of knee troubles throughout his career. Joe later admitted that he shouldn't have played Bunn but start with Roger Palmer instead. However, Frankie had played a big part in the build-up with his six goals against Scarborough.

One thing I noticed during the game was that Cloughy wouldn't let his full backs, Brian Laws and Stuart Pearce, go beyond half way. With it being the hottest day of the year at pitchside and aware of our fixture congestion he was conserving energy. We ran out of it, they scored the goal through Nigel Jemson and took the cup. Despite being behind we pressed and pressed. Their keeper, Steve Sutton, made a magnificent save to deny Palmer who had proved a point by livening things up when he came on.

By the end of the game, Clough had recovered and been allowed on to the front row for the second half. He got hold of Joe at the end, led him off and they had a long chat. Cloughy told Joe that his players were a credit to him and that they had had a fantastic season. They shared a beer in the Forest dressing room while Forest were receiving the plaudits from their supporters out on the pitch. Joe remembered Clough as being lovely and gracious in victory. There was definitely a lot of mutual admiration between the two former strikers but we all knew at this stage that the great man was on his way out. There would be just one more trophy to come for him, the Full Members Cup a couple of seasons later.

After Wembley we were proud of our efforts but there was still a sense of anti-climax because we had failed to put Nottingham Forest away after beating some of the top sides in the country. Joe tried to get across to the lads that they could still push for a play-off place but they were physically and mentally exhausted and just wanted the season to end. Considering that, they did well to finish with two wins and two draws to lose out on a play-off spot by just three points.

The following season, Oldham won the Second Division title and returned to the First Division for the first time in 68 years. We were never out of the top two all season and guaranteed promotion with four games remaining. It took a 92nd minute penalty from Neil Redfearn to come from behind against Sheffield Wednesday and take the Championship trophy, the last match on the plastic pitch. We were great to watch, losing just once at home and finishing top scorers in the league with 83 goals.

We went to the Yew Tree pub some time after getting promoted. Terry Cahill, the Company Secretary, came along with us and took the meeting's minutes. We sat there with sensible heads on while Joe congratulated everyone. Terry emphasised to the group that promotion meant that we now needed a new and totally professional attitude. He wrote words to that effect at the top of the minutes book. When Joe came to look at it later all that Terry had written underneath was a list of the drinks we had bought! By that stage, Terry was sitting in the corner cuddling the charity teddy bear!

Oldham Athletic squad 1991-92, back in the top division for the first time in 68 years. (Picture courtesy of the 'Oldham Evening Chronicle')

Back (left): *Andy Kenton, Greg Wilson, Rob Miller, Andy Holden, Richard Jobson, John Keeley, Jon Hallworth, Paul Gerrard, Brian Kilcline, Ian Thompstone, Mike Fillery, Chris Makin*

Middle: *Billy Urmson (coach), Jim Cassell (chief scout), Paul Moulden, Willie Donachie (player-coach), Frank Bunn, Paul Bernard, Andy Ritchie, Andy Barlow, Rick Holden, Wayne Heseltine, David Currie, Neil Adams, Ronnie Evans (kit manager), Me*

Front: *Nick Henry, Paul Kane, Ian Marshall, Roger Palmer, Joe Royle (manager), Earl Barrett, Graeme Sharp, Mike Milligan, Neil Redfearn*

The top flight brought us into contact with some awesome players. In one of our first games I remember seeing Les Ferdinand warming up for QPR. His calves were bigger than our lads' thighs! Les could leap like a salmon. He got up high and hung there but after an hour he was done, finished. He was substituted a lot because of the energy used in the leaps. Our lads were like pieces of string alongside him.

We kept our place in Division One, finishing 17th in the 1991-92 season and becoming part of the new Premier League the year after. This was a great honour although we only kept it going by the skin of our teeth, staying up for another season with a last-day victory. We felt that we had reached the summit and, after opening his Oldham time in front of 2800 against Shrewsbury, Joe's team regularly attracted crowds of eighteen thousand to Boundary Park.

After starting with players of modest ability I was now working with Oldham lads who were among the best players I've come across throughout my career. Left back Neil Pointon had been at the highest level with Everton and Manchester City before arriving at Boundary Park in 1992. He and Steve Redmond came to shore up the defence for Premier League football, Earl Barrett having moved to Aston Villa. Neil was a very strong lad who could club the ball for miles from left back and was instrumental in Oldham getting to the semi-final of the FA Cup in 1994. We were drawn at Bolton Wanderers in the quarters. Wanderers were so confident about progressing that they had already organised the coaches for the semi-final at Wembley! We spoilt the party and won 1-0. I have never really experienced silence and total disbelief after a game as I did that day. They were convinced they would roll us over.

In truth, Bolton should have been 3-0 up in half an hour. David Lee on the right wing ran riot against Chris Makin. He tore Chris to pieces but his final delivery was wayward. We had a Norwegian lad at right-back, Tore Pedersen. Thor received a bad injury in front of the dug-out, damaging the medial ligaments in his knee. I got hold of his knee and it was wobbling around in my hand. I regularly used an orthopaedic surgeon called Tony Banks who was a season ticket holder at Bolton. Suddenly there was a tap on my shoulder. I looked up to see Tony standing over me! He told me to get Tore sorted for an operation at the Beaumont Hospital in Bolton the next day, Sunday.

One of the great pleasures of working as a physiotherapist in top-level sport has been how it has allowed me to interact with surgeons, doctors and radiologists. I used to get invited to watch operations, follow an MRI scan and see things unfold as the pictures came in. I felt very privileged. There's lots of talk about CPD, Continuing Professional Development, in all types of work. Here, I was witnessing it first-hand.

Back at the Bolton game, Pedersen's injury forced us to re-think. We moved Makin to right back where he normally played and brought Neil Pointon on at left back. Well, Neil terrorised Lee. The two had had dealings in the past. The supply from the Bolton wide-man dried up and we got a foothold, scoring in the second half through Darren Beckford. Sadly, the record books show that we were to miss out on a final for the second time in five years to Manchester United and a goal which was a turning point in the Latics' fortunes. This time our semi-final took us back to Wembley.

Wembley FA Cup Semi-final, April 1994. Mark
Hughes was to wipe the smiles from our faces.

Neil Pointon popped up to give us the lead in front of 56 000 spectators before Mark Hughes wiped it out with a spectacular volley a minute or so from the end of extra time. When we walked off the Wembley pitch, Joe said to me,

'We don't stand a chance in the replay on Wednesday do we?'

I said, 'No.'

We went into the dressing room and the lads had their heads in their hands.

Mark Hughes' goal was to change many lives, kick-starting a decline after years of steady progress. In the replay at Maine Road, United were sneaky. They brought the flying winger Andrei Kanchelskis in and we finished up playing with three full backs! I had to go on at the end of the game and unscrew them from the ground they'd been turned so many times! We failed to win any of our last seven league games and were relegated from the Premier League on the last day of the season after a draw at Norwich City. Starting afresh in the second level, we lost six out of ten games up until the beginning of October. By November 1994, Joe, Willie and I had all left. One defining Mark Hughes moment had such an effect and we had a massive hangover lasting weeks. Ironically, Joe was to return to Wembley a season later and pick up the FA Cup with Everton.

One of the Oldham players involved in the FA Cup disappointment was Andy Ritchie. Every football club has its legendary figures and Andy Ritchie was right up there among Oldham supporters. They even had a song about him, 'Andy Ritchie's Magic.' Andy was a player who I always said had an international touch and non-league legs. He was not the best at running but he had a good brain. There was genuine ability and he could score goals that won important games. Andy came to Boundary Park in 1987. He was 26 but had been around for a long time, making his debut for Manchester United as a teenager. In fact, he scored hat tricks against Leeds and Tottenham as a teenager before, surprisingly, being sold to Brighton. He came to us via Leeds United and we knew we had signed a proven goalscorer. Andy was a fantastic asset—good in the air, a great touch and a lethal finisher. Joe used to play wide men. Rick Holden was on the left, Denis Irwin on the right. Andy got plenty of crosses from those two and he capitalised, scoring 104 goals from 250 games in his Oldham career.

Earl Barrett, Andy Barlow and Andy Ritchie

Unfortunately, Andy spent a lot of time with me. He got more than his fair share of niggles, hamstrings, calves and he even got a bad back from lifting a pram. He suffered from a bulging disc and in the end I got him epidural injections every few months and surgery followed. Altogether, he missed quite a few games. Andy would regularly have me in tears of laughter. He was genuinely one funny lad. We would regularly try and out-do each other and it passed many an afternoon. Facilities were limited and it becomes more difficult to manage players long-term when there's little scope for variety. You have to ask yourself,

'Is it worth doing a hundred press ups or sit-ups for half an hour just to fill in time? Does it make them any better?'

You constantly had to be creative. Some days I would go into the club and tell my group that we were off on a walk and take some money. We'd stop for a coffee. It was a change.

Chapter Twelve

GAMES WITH BIG RON

'Let's go out into the car park and sort it there.'

E very game was a social occasion. My eldest, James, used to go on the pitch with his friends after the home games. I was on my second marriage by then but had James at weekends. No one ever kicked the lads off. I'd be having a drink but would nip out every now and then to make sure they were alright, then it was back into Joe's office.

Joe with my son James (left) and friend, Matt.

These sessions would regularly last until seven 'o'clock then it would be up the road to 'The Old Grey Mare' in Royton for a couple more before going our separate ways. Joe was tolerant of fans to a degree, never openly rude, but often made his excuses and left.

More than likely he would be going out so would nip home to pick his wife up. Next port of call for me was the Maple Squash Club for a drink or two followed by pudding, chips and peas. Jean worked there and after we left it was back home for 'Match of the Day' and bed.

I also used to go to the squash club a lot with the players. I played squash myself and had regular games against Joe. He was like a windmill in the middle of the court! I was always ducking under the massive swings of his racquet. We had some really competitive games, usually after training. Ron Atkinson used to come down as well when he was manager of Manchester United. Joe was very friendly with Big Ron.

Through Ron I got invited to the training ground at the Cliff for Friday night games. He organised them and attracted a lot of former ex-pros including Frank Worthington, Len Cantello, Asa Hartford, Stuart Pearson and Brendan Batson. It was usually ten-a-side indoors on the Astroturf. Joe used to play at centre half alongside Eric Harrison. Eric is best known for being the man behind the Manchester United youth set-up which produced the likes of David Beckham, Ryan Giggs, the Nevilles, Paul Scholes and Nicky Butt.

Ron would invite Sunday League teams and businesses to play against us. He played as well and was hilarious. I was always getting bollocked by him. He would shout to me,

'SOSS, just win the ball and give it to your best player.'

'Who's that, Boss?'

'Me, of course! That's why I brought you in.'

Ron was, and is, a top man. He is definitely one of the funniest fellas I've met in football. I just couldn't imagine him being like he was with us when he was doing the business at Old Trafford. It would have been deadly serious on a match day so for the likes of him and Joe games at the Cliff were a release from constant pressure.

In the end Ron would lean on the wall and watch the game. If we were getting beat he just used to play on. 'Extra time!' he would shout across the pitch. He played on until we got the winner. Afterwards we gathered in Ron's office for a de-brief. There would always be a big pot of tea on his desk. He would analyse the game we had just played as if it had been a cup tie and was more than happy to tell us where we had all gone wrong.

There were so many good players involved. I had a tiff with former United and Scotland winger Willie Morgan once. Willie had been playing for the opposition and I hadn't given him a kick all night. We went in for a ball and I was a bit robust, let us say. We ended up in a tangle. Willie said something and I replied,

'I'm not going to continue in here. If you want to say something let's go out into the car park and sort it there.'

He didn't take me up on the 'offer' and I was left thinking that Ron wouldn't let me continue on a Friday after I had riled a player of Morgan's pedigree. It was a nervy post-match meeting for me that evening. Big Ron turned to me and said,

'Did you offer Willy Morgan outside back there, SOSS?'

'Yes I did, Boss.' I was petrified about what his answer might be because I thought I'd ruined my Friday football. He replied,

'You'll do for me.'

A lad called Ian Seddon stormed off after one of Ron's post-match talks in his office. Ian had played for Bolton among other teams. He organised the Bolton Wanderers veterans team who I turned out for. Ian is a really nice lad but Ron set about him over the cup of tea. He was mischievous and used to set these situations up to deliberately test people out. Seddy didn't take kindly to criticism about his passing and kept saying,

'I'm not having that, no I'm not.' He was under control while he was saying this but in the end he left in a hurry and stormed out. Ron started laughing. We met up with Seddy later in the pub.

'He was bang out of order there,' said Seddy.

'He was only taking the piss, mate,' we replied.

The games tended to work out every other week. Obviously there were times when Oldham were away and on an overnight stop and there were also times when Big Ron was away with United. I always looked forward to them. Big Ron left United in 1986 and this coincided with us getting the plastic pitch at Oldham. I took over the organisation of the matches, we went to eleven-a-side and most of the lads who had played at the Cliff came across to play at Oldham. I spent most of Thursday on the phone sorting my Friday team out! It made me realise how stressful being a manager was! One thing I took into the Oldham games was Ron's habit of extending the game until we had got a result. We also started getting a proper referee organised. I treated a lot of local players and referees so had got to know quite a few. They used to really enjoy it and we had a whip-round afterwards to cover their expenses.

By then others like Martin Buchan had joined us and Joe was now up front. For corners he'd say,

'Just chip it and I'll land on the keeper in the back of the net.'

He used to pile through and ended up in the net with up to three of their players! The games continued to be massively competitive and the fellas who took part were unbelievable. The likes of Len Cantello and Asa Hartford were proper players. Then there was former United legend Stuart Pearson, still an amazing competitor with brilliant one-touch, sharp and strong as an ox. Here I was playing alongside a hero who I had watched score the opening goal which helped Manchester United win the FA Cup against Liverpool in 1977.

When Fergie took over at United he stopped the Friday games. They started up again but it was just for the United staff. Fergie himself turned out every now and then. The lad who organised it was the Cliff groundsman, Ben, who had done it for Ron. We met up and he asked if I fancied taking a team down. We did and we beat them. There was Len and Asa among others. Ferguson didn't like it and told Ben not to invite us again!

We also played some charity games around the country for Ron. We would often travel on United's team coach. Ron gave team talks which were so inspirational that I would have run through the wall to get on the pitch after them . . . and it was just a charity game! I could just imagine what he was like when it was for real.

We played at Oxford United one Sunday. Ron had a lad called Bobby Smith travelling up from Plymouth. Bobby must have caught three or four trains to get there. Ron had the number seven shirt hung up before the game. Bobby prepared to get ready and moved towards hooking it off the peg.

'Stop right there, Bobby, George Best's coming. Yours is over there . . . number 12!'

Bobby was not best pleased and let everyone know.

'All these trains to fucking get here. Up at the crack of dawn only to find that fucking George Best is playing instead of me.' Smith mumbled to himself over and over again. Time moved on and George was nowhere to be seen. Ron would come back in, chipping away at Bobby:

'I know it's getting close to kick off but he's on his way, he's on his way.'

Finally, he just burst out laughing and let Bobby out of his misery about five minutes from kick off. We had all been in on the joke and had kept reporting back to Ron about how Bobby was reacting. Bobby said to anyone who cared to listen, 'I knew he was having me on, I knew George Best wasn't coming all along.'

On the charity games we would often play against kids who wanted to make a name for themselves by putting a foot in. Not a good idea. Our lads would snap them in two, within the laws of the game, of course. They were determined to teach the young upstarts a lesson if the situation demanded it. Worthington, Cantello, Hartford and Pearson were the kind of hardened professionals you just wouldn't mess with. The sort of players you don't see today. They were able to look after themselves in the context of the game. The charity games would end with a few drinks and some fund-raising and were really enjoyable to be involved with.

I also used to play for the Piccadilly All-Stars who ended up as the Manchester All-Stars. This team was made up of actors and former players. There would be a few guys from Coronation Street and Hollyoaks. Phil Middlemiss ('Des Barnes' in Corrie) was the goalkeeper and his mate Gary Webster, from 'Minder' was also a regular. Others from stage and screen included Patrick Robinson, from 'Casualty', Michael Le Vell ('Kevin Webster') and Sean Wilson ('Martin Platt'), both from Coronation Street. Norman Whiteside would also turn-out on behalf of the football fraternity. Mick. the big lad with the beard from Brookside, was a handful up front. We got the 'Pint of Lager and a Packet of Crisps' actor from television while Mike Sweeney, the Manchester DJ, and his mate Tony played because they organised the games. On one occasion, the All-Stars opened the new ground at Colwyn Bay in north Wales. There must have been a couple of thousand watching. At the end the ex-international pro-footballers trudged off for a shower. We looked out and there were all the soap stars still signing autographs. I said to them, 'That used to be you.'

I just loved playing and with Sunday League as well it meant that I often had two Sunday games! One of my most memorable games was for a Joe Royle Celebrity Team against a Middleton and Heywood Police Team in aid of the Birch Incident Fund, set up after the unfortunate death of a policeman. I lined up alongside Kenny Dalglish and Graham Souness! Can't be bad!

Chapter Thirteen

AWAY DAYS WITH ATHLETIC

'You've had the only prawn out of the whole batch
which had drunk nine pints of lager!'

At Oldham you were never far from a party. In fact, Joe called it a 'mobile party' or 'rent-a-party'. At Newcastle and Oldham you were regarded as a hero if you could drink day and night. Beer was freely available on the return from away games. Players got freedom and they respected that. They would bust a gut for the gaffer. Characters such as Mike Milligan, Nick Henry, Ian Marshall, Frankie Bunn, Andy Ritchie and Rick Holden gave it their all both on and off the pitch.

Tuesday Club was a regular for many of the players. We would train and then they would go out on the lash Tuesday night knowing that there was no training on Wednesday. It was not unusual to see them out and about midweek in the pubs and clubs of Oldham. Joe usually knew what his players got up to and they could never work out how he knew where they had been but Oldham was a small town and Joe had mates everywhere. The lads came in one day thinking they had been particularly clever having kept out of the way the day before. What they didn't know was that Joe had the very book in front of him that they all used to sign into a club! You can't stop players if they want a drink and that's fine as long as it's controlled. How could you peg back a mischievous bugger like Milligan who could play football and not let anyone down on the pitch? It was harmless fun much of the time. No one got hurt. Joe always said he was more concerned about where they were physically and mentally come three 'o' clock on a Saturday.

It was a weekly arrangement but Joe eventually had to put an end to it when players started getting themselves into trouble. When Tuesday Club imposes on the smooth running of the club then you have a problem. There were bits and pieces coming out about arguments in pubs and things. Joe certainly wasn't impressed when Tommy Wright drove into three parked cars as he left the club after one session! The lads had gone straight out after training. I was just finishing my duties for the day when Tommy came into my treatment room in shock. It was all sorted out.

When we travelled on a Friday the players would eat at about seven 'o' clock and the staff and directors would meet in the bar. I often missed that because I was attending to players. I might need to give an anti-inflammatory or a sleeping tablet, perhaps a paracetamol. I needed to be there with antibiotics in case a sore throat flared up. I'd ring the club doctor who would tell me what to prescribe.

After the lads had gone to their rooms for the evening we would go out for a meal and a few drinks off site. Willie Donachie in his own mind was still a player and he had a model lifestyle so he would always stay behind and kept an eye on things. As Joe would say,

'We've prepared the lads all week, now it's time for us to have a wind down.'

Joe was a large person physically and instantly recognisable as we toured the country. People were always trying to attract his attention. He was always good with autographs but didn't suffer fools. He didn't need a minder but if he could see a situation brewing he would apologise before departing. He was not one to encourage a confrontation. It would be something along the lines of,

'Nice meeting you, got to go.'

There would be staff, directors, friends and associates of Joe who might be down. Our meal would usually be Italian, Chinese or Indian. We'd eat about nine then it was back to the hotel for eleven-ish. We had a few more drinks then Joe would go to bed at around midnight. Each time he would turn to me and my mates and say,

'If you're in before three 'o' clock in the morning you're sacked!'

I'm convinced that Joe knew every move we were making. We would get a taxi or the hotel minibus. The destination depended on where we were playing the following day. If we were in Waltham Abbey, which we were quite a lot, it was either a club called Hollywood in Romford or the Epping Forest Country Club. These were famous night-spots where the celebs went. If we were in London we would go to Charlie Chan's in Walthamstow. That was like a Bunny Club. Croydon would be the Blue Orchid which was hilarious and we would head there if we were playing at Palace or Wimbledon. It wasn't all down south. We had some great times up north as well. If it was Newcastle it was Julie's by the quay side.

We used to invite people back from the clubs to the hotel. Plates of sandwiches were ordered and the party atmosphere continued. Some of the lads from Manchester would have travelled down under their own steam and bunked up. I regularly took the mattress off my bed and they crashed out on it while I slept on the base. Even long-term injured were allowed to travel and come out. We stayed at Bexleyheath for the Charlton game and went to an Indian restaurant. There was Ronnie Evans, me and two players who were unavailable for selection, Paul Jones and John Kelly. Ronnie had told me he had no money so asked if I would sort the taxi out when we returned to the hotel and he would pay me back the next day.

We were on the way back, worse for wear as ever. I was in the back with the other two and whispered to them to leg it when we got to the hotel. We left Ronnie stranded with no money and headed for the bar for more drinks. After what seemed like an age Ronnie appeared and told us he had given the driver his watch for security. We were pissing ourselves. Joe was quite happy for guys like Paul and John to be around, even when injured because they kept spirits up.

After stitching Ronnie up with the taxi driver we made things worse by putting all our drinks on his room bill. Next morning when he came to pay, we hid round the corner and watched him. In the end we took pity on him and each put £20 in the kitty. With all this going on Ronnie had missed his pre-match meal so he got a prawn sandwich and managed to eat it before we left. He got on to the bus and Ronnie went straight to the toilet to throw up. The bus pulled off and the toilet lid fell, hitting him across the bridge of his nose. He came staggering up the steps with blood running down his face. You just wouldn't want to show yourself in that situation. The players loved it while Ronnie was full of apologies in front of Joe,

'Sorry, Boss, it must have been the prawn sandwich.'

Joe replied, 'You know something, Ron, you must have been unlucky. You've had the only prawn out of the whole batch which had drunk nine pints of lager!'

Very often we didn't have to pay for our hotel drinks, only telephone calls. I would order a couple of bottles of champagne and a plate of sandwiches and charge it to the club. After one journey, Ronnie and I got called into the secretary's office. There was a bill for about £300 on the table in front of us. Various items had been highlighted and I was trying to read it upside down. On the way in Ronnie had said,

'I'm not paying for a thing, we were on club business. They're not going to get me. We're allowed calls home to families.'

I had been ringing girlfriends all night! I told Ronnie to calm down and see what was happening. As I read upside down I could see it wasn't for the drinks. The secretary went on about how it wasn't on to run up bills and Ronnie kept twittering on,

'I'm not paying for a thing.'

I was trying to shut him up. There was £15 of phone calls and £300 in drinks and sandwiches. The secretary seemed to want us to just pay for the calls. I had cottoned on to that but Ronnie hadn't! It was a big relief and I reassured Ronnie that I would cover most of the bill because they were mainly my calls.

'Win or lose, have a booze,' was the motto and we hammered the booze on many occasions, particularly me and Ronnie. The lads would be creasing themselves when we came down to breakfast the next morning!

We surpassed ourselves in Sunderland. We finally got to bed at seven 'o' clock! There were two body-builders in the hotel that night with two birds. I said to Ronnie, 'Watch this'. I ordered two bottles of champagne with four glasses and it didn't take long for the girls to join us, with one of the body builders. The girls tucked in and I sat up all night chatting to them and hoping the body-builders would give up and leave us. Ronnie couldn't last the pace and fell asleep in the early hours. Eventually, I'd had enough, woke Ron and went to bed.

We came down about three hours later at about ten 'o' clock because we had to put the kit out at the ground. We went outside for some fresh air. Joe was out there.

'You two, come here,' he ordered. 'What time did you get to bed last night?'

Ronnie replied straight away, 'Two o'clock, boss.'

'Try again.'

'Three-ish.'

'Try again.'

Once again I read the situation quicker than my mate and said straight away,

'Seven o'clock, boss'.

'I know. I came down early this morning and the guy behind the desk couldn't wait to tell me that two of my players had been in the bar till seven on the morning of a game. I said to him, don't tell me. One's small with dark, curly hair and a moustache and the other's a bit bigger, blond hair and a moustache'

'Spot on.'

Joe's parting shot to us was, 'Come and see me on Monday for a pay rise!' We staggered off up the prom for some fresh air.

I've already mentioned how directors joined us on the lash. Rod Adams lived round the corner from me and was the 'entertainments manager'. He organised where to go and booked taxis. He did it well and was proud of it! Other 'fun guys' included David Brierley and Norman Hogan. The Commercial Manager, Gordon, was yet another who came along. Seats on the away trips were eagerly sought and at a premium.

Chairman Ian Stott also enjoyed the odd night out but he was one of a few directors who never bought a round. Ian was always careful with his money and perhaps didn't take too much cash out with him. A good example of him being reluctant to shell out was the time when I needed an exercise bike for the injured lads to use. I had shown him a catalogue with these all-singing, all-dancing bikes in but he clearly didn't want to pay for one. Instead, he offered me one and presented me with a flimsy ladies exercise bike which belonged to his missus.

'She doesn't use it anymore, Ian, you can have it.'

Well, within three or four weeks the lads had worn the belt down. It was done in and we left in the corner of the gym, a pile of metal. The groundsman happened to be walking by one day and asked if we had any use for it, if not he would scrap it. He threw it in the skip. Come Christmas time Ian Stott approached me and asked for the exercise bike back! I told him it had broken ages ago.

'Right, you'll have to order me another,' he said. It went on the medical bill! I had to put it in the boot of his car and he gave it to his wife for a Christmas present!

I remember Ian getting out of a taxi in Soho one night and staggering off down an alley. Suddenly a crashing noise pierced the air as he walked into some bins. Ronnie said, 'Should we help him?' We thought for a moment and then walked off the other way.

Another director who was a bit tight was Derek Taylor, high up in the Halifax Building Society. I think it was Brighton and it was his round. We were waiting with empty glasses. No luck. We returned to the hotel and he put his room key on the bar. I clocked the number and after he had gone to bed ordered a drink on Derek for us and everyone else in the bar! The hotel staff members were having a bit of a party and appreciated my gesture.

I tried it again another night and ordered a bottle of champagne. Unbeknown to us the bar steward had phoned Derek and said, 'There's two people at the bar trying to put champagne on your room bill.'

'Don't tell me, one's small with dark, curly hair and a moustache.'

'Yeah'

'. . . and the other is taller, blond . . . .'

'Correct.'

'Let 'em have it on me.'

Even the coach driver used to get involved in our nights out and would frequently fall asleep over the bar. We'd say to the bar staff,

'Can we leave him and come back for him later?' Joe could never understand why the driver would allow himself to get involved with us and would regularly state the obvious to him,

'You've got to drive tomorrow.'

We were playing at Swansea and Joe kept saying to the driver all the way down, 'Don't get caught up with the MASH unit.'

'I'm not going near them.'

The lads came down the next morning for a little walk along the beach. As they boarded the coach the driver's looking distinctly shady. In fact he's slumped over his wheel. Joe said, 'Did you?' The driver's reply was, 'Yes'

Joe went on, 'You've got to be careful. There's millions of pounds of talent on this bus and you're driving.'

I chirped up, 'You're right, boss. Jobbo, get off the bus now. You're coming with us. The rest of you can stay on.' Joe thought that was hilarious and kept chuckling about it for some time after. In fact, he still tells the story to this day.

I'm not saying that the driver got drunk. He was a smashing lad who just used to get tired when going out with Ronnie and me, forgetting that we had a totally different resistance to long nights. It became a standard thing away from home. Would the driver be able to keep up with the MASH unit?

Joe has already given his account in his foreword of the time I was arrested. It's not something that I'm proud of. We were in Kensington and doing our usual before the massive occasion at Stamford Bridge to mark our debut in the Premier League on Saturday, August 15th 1992. I had a friend down in London who used to come and see us at the hotel. On this occasion she brought a bottle of champagne. We were at the bar at the time so I said to the girl behind the bar,

'Can you put that in the fridge and we'll have it later?'

I could tell that the barmaid wasn't very pleased with my request. 'You can't do that, you have to buy our champagne.'

'I will be buying yours and I'll pick mine up later if that's ok.'

I had got off on the wrong footing and things were going to get worse. The hotel doubled up as a night club. We did our usual, went out for a meal and a few drinks. Then it was back to the hotel, and Ronnie and I finished up in the night club. We had bought a bottle of champagne earlier and paid the girl behind the bar to open the one we had given her to look after.

Ronnie had fallen asleep at the bar and I went to the toilet. Ronnie used to regularly crash out on the high stools with his chin in his hand. When I came back he was getting thrown out by bouncers. I went over and, unfortunately, diplomacy goes out of the window with me after a few drinks. I got embroiled in an argument and next thing I know I've been thrown down the stairs and been pinned to a wall by a bouncer. My next recollection was coming round in the back of a police car. I think I had been 'choked off' by a bouncer, his arm across my throat. I asked what I was doing in the police car and was told that I'd head-butted the duty manager.

'I haven't. I can't have,' I protested. 'I got thrown out of the night club, pinned against the wall and next thing I'm being taken away in a police car.' I was locked up and in my stupor I fell asleep on the slab. I was woken by the door opening, light filling the room and the beam being obliterated by this big shadow. It was Joe. He was in no mood for a discussion so I followed his instructions and it was clear he wanted to get me away as fast as possible.

I meekly went away and back to bed in the hotel. The next morning Joe came to see me with Rod Adams. Rod believed me about the alleged head-butt, Joe didn't. It would be more difficult to cover up such an incident in today's game. It would be flashed up on Sky Sports News and be online in the newspapers. I could have ended up in court, charged and probably out of a job.

I still maintain that I didn't do anything wrong. I had loads to drink, admittedly, but no marks on my head. I rang the duty manager to offer him two tickets for the game. I wanted to apologise in person and hand the tickets over. He was guarded on the phone and didn't take up the offer. He said that I had broken his nose. No way could I have struggled past that bouncer, physically pushed him to one side and nutted the duty manager.

Joe had been very helpful, supporting me to the nth degree. I could tell he wasn't too happy about it. It wasn't one of my greatest moments. I made mistakes at Oldham but was fortunate because Joe always protected me. The events of that night didn't help my cause with some of those high up at the football club as, inevitably, news spread and it was one factor which ultimately led to my departure.

All good things come to an end and my boss and good friend eventually left Boundary Park. Joe was lured away from Oldham in November 1994. He went back to Goodison Park and in his first season took Everton to the FA Cup glory that had been within touching distance for the Latics. Graeme Sharp took over from Joe. Graeme was a smashing bloke and great player. He had come to Oldham when we were promoted to the old Division One and his goals and experience were instrumental in keeping us in the top league when the new Premier League was formed. Graeme had three years on the pitch before a back injury finished him with sciatica down one leg. His qualities were all-too-obvious. He was strong, good in the air and had a very good touch. To look at him it made you wonder what he was like in his prime. He was, of course, an Everton legend. They liked their number nines at Goodison, much as they did at Newcastle.

On top of all this, Graeme was a very generous and thoughtful guy. On the end of season holidays in Tenerife or Magaluf he would say to me and my assistant,

'Don't book anything tomorrow, you are out with me.' He showed his appreciation for what we had done by treating us for the day, an unbelievable gesture.

Chapter Fourteen

JOY AND DISAPPOINTMENT

'I think we need a parting of the ways,'

The ups and downs of football were perfectly demonstrated in a few short months during 1994. We had gone from the high of reaching the FA Cup semi-final to relegation from the Premier League. My own fortunes rose again when Bryan Hamilton rang me. We had met up four years earlier for a one-off match between an Irish League and a Football League side at Windsor Park in Belfast. We had a very experienced team including the likes of Bruce Grobbelaar, Gary Pallister, Matt Le Tissier and Peter Reid and it was a brilliant occasion. I've got a big engraved crystal bowl at home to commemorate the event. I particularly remember Liverpool's keeper, Bruce Grobelaar. Size-wise he was enormous. You didn't get that indication on TV. He was tall and larger-than-life yet a real gentleman. Bruce's ability was top class. He used to pluck crosses off people's heads one-handed!

Bryan Hamilton had gone on to get the Northern Ireland position. He rang Joe to see if he would be prepared to release me part-time to be his physio alongside my work with Oldham Athletic. Joe said, 'No problem'. We were in Tenerife, drowning our sorrows after relegation, when Bryan rang.

Bryan told me of a tour of a Northern Ireland tour to America in June to play some warm-up games with teams ahead of the World Cup over there in 1994. Northern Ireland hadn't qualified but would provide good opposition to some of those who had. I was delighted to accept his invitation and to get the chance to add international football to my CV.

We played in the American Football stadiums. The first match was against Colombia just outside Boston. Colombia was enjoying its strongest period in the nineties and had qualified for the World Cup unbeaten including a historic 5-0 win over Argentina in Buenos Aires. Not many have done that!

Perhaps my biggest fascination with the game was the chance to see the legendary Carlos Valderrama close up. He was renowned for his shock of blond afro hair as much as his mesmerising technique and a flamboyant style! At half time I followed him down the tunnel and had to control myself to avoid rubbing my hand through his hair to see what it felt like!

The Northern Ireland team didn't get a touch for twenty minutes. It was just pass-pass-pass from the South Americans and it was brilliant to watch. International football is all about passing the ball and the Colombians did it with such skill. They looked certainties to go through to the final stages of the World Cup but didn't get beyond the qualifying group. Defeats by Romania and the United States were to seal their fate.

Defender Andrés Escobar attempted to cut out a cross against the States but accidentally deflected the ball into his own net. Soon after returning to Colombia, Escobar was shot dead, an act allegedly connected to his error. Apparently the country's football was run by drug cartels and they had massive money on their team to do well.

From Boston we moved to New York and got a free weekend after the game was called off. This gave us a chance to do all the sight-seeing. We were invited out to see the Statue of Liberty, have a meal and enjoy a cabaret. There were plenty of characters in that Irish team and the sing-songs were brilliant! A good number of the lads went into management. Nigel Worthington, Iain Dowie, Steve Lomas, Gerry Taggart, Jimmy

Quinn and Jim Magilton all carried their experience on after retiring from the playing side.

It was a great honour to be involved. Hamilton let me take part in warm-ups and join in practice. One of my major roles was to provide drinks, not the alcoholic type on this occasion! It was so hot that tubs of iced water were provided round the grounds. The heat was particularly noticeable in Miami where Mexico beat us before we returned home. We had about five nights there and it was a real eye-opener. For a start I'd never seen so many barely-clothed girls in one place. Everywhere you looked there were thongs! There were loads of live bands on and not just run-of-the-mill. There were some brilliant musicians. We went out one night and this girl came into the bar with hardly anything on—and a live python round her waist! There was a noticeably wide circle round her. Gerry Armstrong said,

'Don't look now but there's a snake behind you.' I turned and this massive beast was about a metre away from my face! I've never seen anything like it. Gerry was a big mate of mine. We were party animals and kindred spirits.

Miami was just totally wacky. We were made aware that if we wandered off the main strip we could be in danger. In fact, there was a knifing just round the corner while we were there.

I arrived back in August to be met with news of a story about me in the News of the World. It was something along the lines of, 'PHYSIO HAS BALL WITH PLAYER'S WIFE'. I had split up from Jean, my second wife, in the January. Christine, who was later to become my third wife, had split from her husband, David, in the June of the previous year. Her husband had put the story in to the paper. When it says he was a player he was connected with a Sunday League side and he never actually played! He used to come and watch the games. We'd go to the pub after and I think that's where I met Christine. Joe Royle was partial to eating a carnation at the time and she sold flowers. On a Sunday David would bring flowers in after the game to see if he could sell any. I offered to buy some and promptly ate one. She made a bee-line for me but I resisted,

'I know your husband and I'm married anyway.'

A few months after she had split from her husband Christine rang me and asked for some match tickets. I said I'd sort it. I told her to come and pick the tickets up at the ground. I could then run my eye over her and see how she was looking these days. Anyway, she turned up and the rest was history.

The paper made a story and printed it on something like page 34. The gist was that I'd tried to split them up. The only bit of truth in the whole article was describing me as a 'good midfield player'! It mentioned the Northern Ireland tour in America and said that we played against West Germany and someone else. They had made the names up. There was also a large photograph of me taking an Oldham player off the pitch. I was really annoyed and determined to take action. My solicitor rang me on the day it was in, laughing,

'We'll make a few bob here.'

I said, 'Do what you want.'

Dad wasn't happy either. He didn't approve of my lifestyle anyway. I couldn't really care to be honest. I just rampaged through my life with little respect for anyone. This was at odds with the caring profession that I had chosen where I gave everything for my patients and players. It's only looking back that I am prepared to concede that I was wrong at times and I am sorry for the distress that the newspaper coverage caused Mum and Dad.

After the article came out, Bryan rang and said there was concern within the Northern Ireland management about the story. I explained that there should be no problem and described the circumstances. I added that it wasn't true and that I was suing the paper. Bryan was sympathetic but they had a vote on the Northern Ireland committee and it went against me. As there was no international action for a while, I didn't find out until the following January.

In the end I got £15000 and a small apology hidden in the newspaper. By November I had lost my job with Oldham as past misdemeanours caught up with me.

My time working alongside Graeme Sharp at Boundary Park was short-lived. When Joe left bound for Everton he warned me to watch my back. He said,

'Look I can't take you with me, they've got a physio at Goodison.'

He wasn't a sacking man anyway was Joe.

'If an opportunity comes along I'll give you a ring. That's the best I can do.'

He added a word of caution, 'Just a warning. They're after you here. I've looked after you until now but I can't do that anymore.'

Dad kept warning me as well. In all honesty, I had been a bit wild at times at Oldham, regularly getting into scrapes with local police, referees and the FA. I'll tell you more about that later! I don't suppose the incident when I was arrested in London helped either. In the end my chickens came home to roost.

In Graeme's second game in charge Gunnar Halle got sent off for allegedly kicking out. The Norwegian full-back was one of our finest players in our Premier League days and did not have a bad bone in his body so this was an exceptional situation. As he came off we decided to make a substitution. You held numbers up in those days and I used to have a trick. If I threw the numbers at the turf they would stick. On this occasion, they bounced on to the pitch. I had gone up the few steps to the dug-out at Oldham. A policeman told me to go and get the numbers. I said that I couldn't go on to the field without the referee's permission. He obviously didn't know the laws and pursued his argument. I continued to say, 'I can't'. I was in trouble with the police again and had to go in front of the Chief Constable. Fortunately, he accepted my explanation but they were obviously keeping a close eye on me, knowing my reputation.

The following day, Ian Stott called me in to the board room.

'I think we need a parting of the ways,' was his opening statement.

'You going somewhere Chairman?' was my not-very-tactful reply.

'We can't keep having these incidents,' he continued to say.

I pursued my rather flippant line, 'Did I send the wrong numbers on?' By now I realised I was in a serious situation.

'If you pay up my contract I will go,' I told him.

'What contract?' he asked. I had just signed one in the summer. He was Chairman of the football club and didn't know. He had a look at it and I went back the following day. I was offered the equivalent of three months money. I was thinking to myself,

'It's the end of November. I'll not get another job until July next year.'

His offer needed to be six months money to help me through. I dug my heels in and was not amenable. I mentioned getting my solicitor in. He was suing the News of the World at the time!

In the space of a few months I was relegated with Oldham, had the sweetener of the Irish job, the downer of the newspaper article, the end of my contract with Oldham and the termination of my employment with Northern Ireland. Apparently, at his first meeting, the directors told Graeme to go after they'd finished discussing business with him. After he had left the room, they took a vote on me, with two directors missing who would have backed me, and got rid of me.

The Oldham issue went to a tribunal and I got my six months but had to give half to the solicitor. I was trying to prove a point though and had got another job by then anyway. A friend in the Beaumont Hospital in Bolton had offered me some work. It was nice to have a break from the game. I was in a very good department but it was just one room and there were no windows. This was quite a contrast from the life I had been used to—plenty of travelling and lots of fresh air.

I was once told never to stay more than six years anywhere. I had ten and a half at Oldham and if I could spend a single day back in any of the clubs I have worked in I would pick Oldham Athletic. While I was there I had the chance to go to Anfield under Graham Souness. Money talked in the game and the offer was tempting but they couldn't match my combined wage for physio work and running the clinic at Boundary Park. Also, I couldn't see any club able to match the spirit that we had under Joe Royle.

Being in the game has produced a pressure cooker atmosphere for years. The length of the season and the nature of the job meant that I could never have a normal relationship at home. There was a lot of time spent away. I often felt that pressure in my career but never at Oldham. You knew that Joe would get it right and the ride was brilliant. Granted we had a very understanding Chairman in Ian Stott, despite how it ended for me, but Joe would have been like that anywhere. I wasn't surprised when he went on to get further success at Everton, then on to Manchester City.

Chapter Fifteen

MOVING ON

'I was put in charge of Jaffa Cakes, bananas and pasta'

I was playing with Bolton Wanderers vets team at the time. There was Frank Worthington, Paul Mariner, Sam Allardyce, Phil Brown and Alan Kennedy among others. Not bad, eh? It was a privilege to be involved. Frank Worthington was right up there ability-wise and a real crowd pleaser. He had talent in abundance. One trick was to run at someone, get the ball in between his legs then flick it behind, over his head and over his opponent's head. It was a favourite of charity and friendly fixtures but Frank also tried it occasionally in league games. The opponent loses sight of the ball so is confused. Before he knows it, Frank's run round him and off. Paul Mariner was in his late 30s or early 40s but still a fantastic player. The pace had gone but you could see by the things that he could still do that he would have been unstoppable ten years earlier in his prime.

Sam Allardyce spoke to me one Sunday. His physiotherapist at Blackpool was leaving and going to Bradford. He asked if I was interested in the job and I jumped at the chance. Sam and assistant manager Phil Brown were my sort of characters and we got on well. I went to Blackpool in March 1995. It was to be a brief stay by the seaside. I left in June.

I had no quibble with the wage but Chairman Owen Oyston wanted me to live in Blackpool, set up a clinic at Bloomfield Road and to have a share in it. I told Sam that I didn't need to set up a clinic. I already had one in Manchester and it would take two years to get a new one going. I was also reluctant to move my family and kids from Manchester. Sam said, 'Let's just tell him you are looking for a house.'

I had been used to the training ground at Squires Gate as a youngster and my first impression was that it hadn't changed! Big Sam's managerial style impressed me and his later success in the role hasn't surprised me. He regularly asked me how Joe would have done something or other and was the first manager I worked with to use a flip chart. Through it he would show the shape of the team and the tactics as well as the likely shape of the team you were playing. He would flip the pages over to demonstrate our free kick routines and the free kicks we were likely to face. We would be shown who would mark where. It was all very well-organised. He always did his homework. I wasn't there long but I enjoyed my short time at Bloomfield Road. There were some very good players at the club, including the likes of Andy Morrison and Andy Preece.

Try as I might I couldn't strike a deal with Owen Oyston. He had certain ingrained ideas and just wouldn't budge over the basic issues that divided us. Sam used to say,

'I'll speak to him about it. Leave it with me, SOSS.'

After training I'd say to Sam, 'Did you speak to Oyston?'

'No, I couldn't. He had a heavy night last night,' and the chance would pass.

I was to leave Sam in the lurch and he was none too happy about it. He went to America in the summer break and while he was away I got a phone call from Stoke City. Stoke were in the second level at the time, at the Victoria Ground under manager Lou Macari. I decided I had nothing to lose so would ask for everything at interview. They'd probably say, 'No,' and it would be, 'Thank you but no thank you'.

I was interviewed by the Chief Scout and the Chief Executive, Jez Moxey. There was a permanent deal on offer and I asked for a car. I was able to continue living in Manchester although the journey wasn't straightforward, cutting through town to get to one of the busiest sections of the M6. I accepted the job. It was a concrete deal and nothing was left up in the air. It was a promising start.

I had let Sam down but it worked out all right for him in the end because there was a lad called Mark Taylor who lived in Blackpool but was working at Wrexham and desperate to get a job locally. He was appointed and got on so well with Sam that he followed him around as Sam went on to bigger and better appointments after eventually losing his job at Bloomfield Road.

I had two years with Lou Macari at Stoke. Lou was something else. A legendary player, he definitely had his own style of management. Basically, he never trusted any of the players. He was always on their case:

'I could work with you all day and I can't make you better but I can make you fitter.'

I saw the look on the players' faces and knew that they were thinking it was going to be all run, rabbit, run. I knew that players could be made better technically from what I'd seen on the plastic pitch at Oldham and I would take issue with Lou about that.

Lou didn't do much tactically. I remember Paul Peschisolido, our Canadian striker, one day in training. Lou shouted across to him,

'Move, Pesch.'

Pesch looked over and asked, 'Where to?'

'Any bloody where.'

Lou and I clashed a lot. He didn't believe anyone was injured and I fell out with him many times. I don't think he had a high opinion of physiotherapists. I felt that this attitude was making my own position vulnerable as I could be liable to a case of neglect. One day I stormed off having had enough. I got a phone call from Jez Moxey at Knutsford Service Station on the M6. He suggested a meeting with Lou and him in the morning. I'd cooled down a lot by then and agreed. Lou said,

'I'm not going to change.'

I replied, 'I'm not going to change either. You need to know when players are genuinely unfit for insurance purposes.'

As far as I was concerned, Lou was undermining my profession. The three of us sorted things out to an extent. I made it clear to Lou that he needed to respect my opinion when players were unfit. He understood where I was coming from and added that he was prepared to sign anything I wanted to cover me,

'If you tell me it's a four week injury I'll sign to that effect but I'll still end up doing things my way. At least you're covered.'

For the first time I got days off but I'm not sure that they did me any good. Lou would look after the injured players in my absence and the next day was always carnage because he would have made everyone train and run them ragged. It was great to get the time off but it sometimes seemed more trouble than it was worth as I patiently picked up the pieces. Justin Whittle was a case in point. He had been out with a calf strain. Lou had made him do laps and put him out for another month. I saw Justin as a big, tough centre-half, ex-Army but he said,

'I just couldn't say no to him and did what he asked.' I told him he should have made it clear that he couldn't run because of the calf problem. I went in to the players on one occasion and told them,

'I've tried to battle for you but you are going to have to battle for yourselves. If you are unfit to play what's the worst that can happen to you. He can't sack you because you are on a contract, the PFA will support you. He might fall out with you but you have to man-up and look after yourselves.'

Alongside his problem with injured players, a hard core of drinkers also drove Lou mad. He was tee-total, preferring to have a flutter at the bookies instead. He'd have lads who regularly rang up on Monday with mysterious dental appointments. Lou knew they would have been out on the lash and used to fine them two week's wages. They were stopping him from doing what he wanted to do with them. The PFA got involved, explaining to him that he could only fine them one day's wage because that's all they'd missed. With the manager's attitude to drinking, away days were a bit quiet for me after the highs of Oldham. I would often finish up on my own in a hotel bar having a couple of drinks. I might get into a conversation or two but frequently I would be up to bed about nine. That's no good for me. I needed to see a bit of life.

Lou had a defensive mindset. His aim was to keep it tight and nick a goal, unlike previous managers I'd worked with where it was all about scoring more than the opposition. Stoke had some really strong players who put his theory into practice. The back four were gruesome! Ian Cranson, with two bad knees, could head to half-way from the penalty area. Vince Overson, right back Ian Clark and left back Lee Sandford made up a formidable back line. I've seen many a forward get battered down the middle before moving wider to get clattered by Lee or Ian.

Lou got sides revved up and in your face. We reached the play-offs in season one. Leicester beat us 1-0 after we drew 0-0 at Leicester. We had chances to go three nil up away from home. I thought that the home game was a real opportunity but Lou picked a defence-minded, unadventurous team. I said after the game, 'Why?' Lou used to watch games all the time and went into Europe regularly. He replied,

'Teams in Europe will sit in and play for penalties if they play teams they don't expect to beat. It's their only chance.' That's what he tried against Leicester. We had a lot of players the wrong side of thirty in the side at Leicester. The second leg was on the Wednesday, just three days later.

'Those players gave me everything on the Sunday. They hadn't got the legs to repeat the effort so I had to be cautious and I took a chance on the game going to penalties.'

It was certainly not my way of thinking at all but as I watched more European games I thought, 'He's right.' This is what happened. In the play-off second leg, Leicester's Parker scored and our plan went out of the window.

In many respects Lou got success by getting that Stoke team into the play-offs. The next season saw a number of players leave because of the financial situation. There were no funds for the players he wanted. Injuries added to the toll. Big Vince was one, Simon Sturridge another. Simon was a really good striker, a clever player. He battled back from an anterior cruciate ligament injury then did his other one.

Chic Bates was Lou's assistant then there was Ashley Grimes. Ashley was youth team coach and we all worked together. I was still reasonably fit and playing Vets as well as driving back up the M6 on Friday nights for football at the Cliff. Despite Alex Ferguson not wanting me and my team back I managed to infiltrate their staff team! It was not quite the same as in Big Ron's day but still enjoyable.

I was actively involved in the training at Stoke as well as doing my physiotherapy work. Chic would lead or bring up the rear and me the opposite on runs. If there was a five-a-side Lou got everyone involved. There would be no rules. It wasn't unusual to have fifteen-a-side with just two goals. There would be no markers for width. The players would be miles away on the other side and I'd say to Lou,

'You not going to get them back?'

'Nah, leave them alone, they're running around.' That's all he appeared to be interested in.

Lou's departure from Stoke in 1997 coincided with the club's last year at the Victoria Ground. There was less success and a mid-table finish. Lou decided to quit, just as I'd got used to him! I had two years at the Victoria Ground with the passionate Stoke fans. When they sang the old Tom Jones hit, 'Delilah', the hairs on the back of my neck stood on end. It made for an electric atmosphere. The song would start in one section of the crowd and spread, as if it had been rehearsed.

When we moved to the Britannia Stadium the fans were further away, separated from the pitch by one of those tartan all-weather surfaces. Mike Pejic, the coach, used it as a running track. The lads hated it! The Britannia move was exciting for me because I was asked to design the gym and the physiotherapist's room. I was the only physio, as I had been at Newcastle. I made it open plan, the treatment room and gym together with a separate office. It meant that I could treat the players while watching others on the bikes and other equipment.

The Britannia Stadium, Stoke (courtesy of stadiumguide.com)

You spend the first hour to an hour and a half every day treating players. Then they would leave your room at, say, half nine to do rehab work. I'd tell them to do their work but would then find them having a cuppa or reading the paper. Not all of them but, let's face it, it's human nature. If I had everything in one room I could keep my eye on them. My plans went through. It was an exciting move and very much a new start with a new manager. Chic Bates was promoted and brought in Alan Durban as his assistant. As well as being a legendary player at Derby County, Alan had managed teams for about thirteen years so came in with massive experience.

We made a really good start to the 1997-98 season. We were sixth by October and everything was going well. The atmosphere was not as intense at the new stadium but we were getting results, which was the main thing. Then, from October to January, we didn't win a game. We were on Sky in January against Birmingham and they beat us 5-1. It's a fixture which is very much classed as a local derby and it didn't go down well. Our fans were so angry that they invaded the lounge next to the boardroom. Stoke fans can be angry when roused. The board locked themselves in the boardroom while furniture was overturned in the lounge. Bates went and was replaced by Chris Kamara who returned ten years after arriving as a player.

I had so nearly met up with Chris the player at Oldham Athletic. We were having a typical mini-crisis at Boundary Park and he who would have suited us. Joe met him on the motorway. Well, you've seen Chris's face on the telly when the towel drops in the advert. Joe tells me it was like that when he offered him a drop in wages to move from Leeds! Joe explained to Chris that it was our wage scale but he would at least be playing and he wasn't getting a game at Leeds. The move didn't happen.

Chris loved himself so much and although I didn't have anything against him personally it wasn't to work out. It was a bad stage in my career. The secretary of the club, Mike Potts, died of cancer. Mike was a big man and a fantastic fella. His death shocked the whole club. Mike was a mainstay who would sort anything out for you, including lending you money until you were paid. We missed him terribly. Mike's death coincided with Chris Kamara taking over. The secretary had the pleasure of occupying the biggest office at the new ground. Chris Kamara moved in straightaway and it angered a number of employees from the start.

My first encounter with Chris was in the gym and it wasn't the best of starts. I was with the injured players and one thing that was important to me was always getting involved in what I asked them to do. I tried to lead by example. If they were told to do 10k on a bike I did the same. I must admit it's not been as easy as I've got older but I always tried to adopt the principle, 'If I can do it, you can.' If it was 2k on the rowing machine I would hop onto the next machine and get stuck in while they were moaning and groaning.

I had set them a circuit in the gym. The lads had finished and I was on the running machine not far behind them. They were lying around lathered in sweat. Kamara came in and called me across. He said that it wasn't right that I was working when the players weren't. I explained why I did it that way and he clearly didn't agree with me. He just didn't see it. A few days later the youth team coach couldn't come in to work. One of others said, 'SOSS will do it.'

'He's paid to be the physio,' was Kamara's reply.

Every day at 4 pm I would have to report on progress during the day with the injured players. With Chic and Lou they would often say, 'You can push off now,' at about three o'clock. It could be difficult up the M6 as the traffic built up towards the end of the afternoon. I respected Kamara's wish to hold back until four 'o' clock but one day I was still waiting at twenty to five. I said to Mike Pejic, 'I'm out of here'.

'You can't.'

'Watch me,' I replied. 'He's not taking the piss out of me'. I was driving home past Knutsford services when I got a call from Mike.

'He wants you here, mate.'

'Tell him I'm not returning now. I'll see him in his office at nine o'clock in the morning.'

I went in the following day and had it out with the manager. He never gave me an excuse as to why he had kept me waiting. I told him that he was disrespectful and should at least let me know if he was delayed or couldn't make it. 'You do what I say,' was his attitude and then he started to tell me how he didn't like the open-planned room that I had designed and that he wanted to change it. I said, 'Good luck,' before telling him that I had designed it after 16 years experience and that it was done deliberately so that I could oversee up to fifteen players at one time, two on beds and the rest working.

'I'm going to change it anyway,' was his reply.

At that point I thought that he was either going to sack me or that I would leave at the end of the season. I was taken away from what I was used to. I was put in charge of Jaffa Cakes, bananas and pasta meals after the game. That's all he used to say,

'Have you got the Jaffa Cakes . . . ?'

We had gone from an era when Lou Macari wouldn't have the likes of Jaffa Cakes or bananas anywhere near the dressing room and now the place was full of them!

I must admit that I'm deliberately painting the negative side of Chris Kamara. He was ok but we just clashed. Chris had experienced managerial success at Bradford but this part of his career was clearly not going to work out. One thing I will say. There's no doubt that he and his coach revolutionised training. There was a buzz again. Warm-ups, quick feet, change of direction, pace, more ball work. These were all good things which made the lads enjoy training but, unfortunately, they didn't take it on to the pitch. They just didn't perform. Chris had boldly stated that he would build a squad good enough to take Stoke into the Premiership. That claim wasn't helped when one of our only players of real value, Andy Griffin, was sold to Newcastle United. I remember a dressing room address where Chris said,

'You won't like the feel of relegation. Trust me. I've experienced it five times.' I think he said five. I had to leave the room to stop myself laughing.

We didn't win in thirteen games. During that time the club became a hive of activity. Players were coming and going, there were agents aplenty. Neville Southall was brought in. Nev's reactions had gone but he was unbelievable in training. I kept my distance not wanting a repeat of the painful incident against Winsford United all those years ago! Southall was by then an Everton legend and nearing the end of a glorious career but the instant impression was still positive. I had never seen a goalkeeper train as hard as he did. He did not stay at the club for long but was totally dedicated and I was fascinated as I watched him go through his paces. He was a fantastic example of where hard work can get you.

Chris Kamara was sacked in April 1998 and Alan Durban came back with Chic as his assistant. There was a great atmosphere again round the club but, sadly, it wasn't enough to prevent us going down. The final game of the season was against Manchester City at home. We lost 5-2, I think. Both teams went down and both sets of fans showed their displeasure in violent scenes outside the ground. It was one of those strange games for me personally. Joe was manager of City and I went out with him and his staff for a drink after the game. They were all mates of mine. I had made my mind up that I would leave Stoke City at the end of the season. I had had enough. Unbeknown to Stoke I had sorted out another job as the Beaumont Hospital in Bolton had kindly stepped in again.

Brian Little was appointed as new manager at the Britannia. I was summoned to meet him and arrived in a brightly-coloured shirt, shorts and flip flops. He sat in his suit looking at me as if I was off another planet! I was on holiday, though, and in my mind I wasn't going back. Stoke were still unaware of my future plans.

A month after meeting Brian Little, Jez Moxey rang and asked me to come in because Little wanted to know where his physio was. Well, I was taking full advantage of an eight week break. I had sent the injured lads to Lilleshall and made the necessary arrangements for my new job at Beaumont. Moxey said, 'Sorry, but Brian wants to bring his own physio in.'

I said, 'Fine, how much are you going to pay me?' We came to an agreement and I went to Beaumont Hospital. Soon after I was asked by a friend of mine if I would do some work at Altrincham Football Club in Greater Manchester for him as he was going away for a while.

It was part-time and I remained there for the rest of the 1998-99 season. Altrincham were one level below the Conference.

It was just down the road and I did a full year at hospital, amounting to about twenty hours a week plus Altrincham and my own private work. I jumped on the Metro at Middleton and made it to the ground in no time at all. Altrincham was a very well-run club and I really enjoyed it. They have had some proud moments, particularly as FA Cup giant-killers. I still go down and watch them when I can. It was nice to remain in football in some capacity. Bernard Taylor, the manager, was a local character, assisted by Graham Heathcote. Graham had been there a long time. It was a successful season which ended in promotion.

One lad who I came across for the second time was Mark Ward. Wardy had cost Joe Royle eight grand from Northwich Victoria. Joe had gone to watch him and the stand was full of scouts. He left after about twenty minutes. It got back to the local paper who printed that we weren't interested. In fact it was quite the opposite. Joe told me he'd never seen a non-league player like him. Mark had talent, availability and ease on the ball. He had only been at Oldham for a year or two before we sold him for quarter of a million to West Ham.

Altrincham had started the season with Andy Dibble in goal, Brian Kilcline in defence and Nigel Gleghorn in midfield. They didn't win a game for about five. I went in one day and they'd all gone. The gaffer had brought Mark Ward in. We went on a twenty game unbeaten spell. Wardy ran the show from midfield.

I went into the summer break and started to make some enquiries about jobs. Altrincham would have liked me to carry on but Burnley's assistant manager Sam Ellis rang and asked me if I could go to Turf Moor for a chat with manager Stan Ternent.

Chapter Sixteen

BURNLEY—A WRIGHT GOOD TIME

'Climb up the ivy, SOSS, and see if he's in.'

I was interviewed by Stan and the club doctor. They offered me a job and a new era began for me in 1999. It was a full-time position. Stan said,

'I can't offer you much money but I can give you an assistant and I know you do private work.'

That assistant was Nicky Reid, the former Manchester City and Blackburn Rovers defender who had studied for a part-time degree in Sports Rehabilitation at the University of Salford. I worked at Turf Moor between nine and three then got away to do my own practice. Wednesday was a day off for players so I was in between nine and one.

I took warm-ups before the game and joined in occasionally in training. Stan was a stickler and you had to follow his methods. As a medical man you are answerable to a manager who isn't medically trained and you need him to be sympathetic. Arthur Cox and Lou Macari weren't always that way inclined while Stan was intolerant at first. He ruled with an iron grip and we clashed a few times. This is not to say that he wasn't caring and protective. However, he was later to use the following introduction,

'This is SOSS, the best physiotherapist I've ever worked with.'

Joe Royle, on the other hand, would say,

'This is SOSS. You should have seen the state of him last night.'

Joe Royle's sense of humour was bringing smiles to faces yet again but his comment helped fuel a reputation that I had in the game for being a touch mad. To be fair to Joe, if you quizzed him further he would always give the right impression of me. In fact he was instrumental in getting me the Burnley job because Stan rang him up. Joe said that as a physio he couldn't get any better.

Burnley was, and is, an absolutely fantastic club. It was a genuinely warm and happy place to be. We had great success during my five years there. The first year saw us promoted to the First Division. Ian Wright came from Celtic for the last three months of that season and the whole place took off. Stan knew Ian from his time at Crystal Palace. He was Steve Coppell's assistant in the Wright and Bright period when they were a really good side.

One feature that sets top-class strikers apart is their ability to look after themselves. The game used to be more physical in those days and players like Ian Wright were targeted by many an uncompromising defender. Wrighty gave back more than he got and, I'll be honest, before his arrival at Turf Moor I didn't like him all that much because he was always roughing up my players. He was an absolute handful, an all-action player who would snap round the heels of defenders all the time.

Ian gave Richard Jobson a particularly torrid time on one occasion at Oldham. Unsurprisingly, the Oldham fans were heckling him every time he touched the ball and there was a big kerfuffle at the end of the game. He was booed as he left the pitch and then it started to kick off between fans, stewards and Ian in the tunnel. Jobbo was there with his fat lip and bloodied nose where Ian had got him and it all became a bit unsavoury.

Ian Wright had that capacity to wind people up and get under their skin. For want of a better word he was a bit of a 'nark'. When that nark's on your team, though, everything's just fine! I saw a completely different side to Ian when he came to Burnley.

He didn't always play but every time there was an important game he had an influence with goals or assists. His passion for the game was still there. He was hungry. Although undoubtedly larger-than-life he trained hard and his presence in the dressing room gave everyone a massive lift. At Palace, according to Stan, they couldn't get him off the training ground.

Wrighty would set up a situation in training with a keeper and a centre half. The ball would be played out wide and crosses would come in. Ian's movement was amazing. He would take two steps forward. The centre half would track him then Ian would peel off round the back. Even though the defender knew what he was doing he still couldn't handle it. Ian would go two paces back before darting forward again to completely wrong-foot the defender. Those sessions showed me a lot about the skill of a top striker.

Despite being known as a lethal finisher, Ian worked tirelessly for his team. If one moment in a game was to sum up his quality it was at Oxford United. We really needed to win to maintain momentum but the game was dying a death. Ian Wright came on. There was a long, diagonal ball played out to the left corner flag. It was going out of play. Wright chased it, slid in, caught it just before the line, scooped it round in one movement and stood up. An Oxford player had tracked him but Wright got inside him. He crossed to Paul Weller on the far post, Weller finished it off and we won 1-0. That single act summed up everything about Ian Wright. He had the ability, as with other great players, to take a game by the scruff of the neck and change it. I've worked with countless players and very few could do that.

At the end of the 2000 season we were promoted from Division Two. The team travelled to Vilamoura in Portugal for a break. We had got into the air but had to come back to Manchester because one of the wheels wouldn't go up. We sat in the lounge waiting for another plane. Ian Wright goes off and returns with one of the biggest ghetto blasters you've seen resting on his shoulder! The music was soon blasting out! He cranked the atmosphere up and other passengers joined in until the authorities told him to turn it down. He ended up getting us into a private room. It was a long delay of about six hours and Wrighty relieved much of the tension. Ian retired from Burnley after an operation on his ankle and headed for a TV career.

A decade or so later, I was travelling south with Fleetwood Town. We stopped off at MK Dons ground in Milton Keynes for a training session and who should bob up but Ian Wright! He had been appointed as a forwards coach and as soon as he saw me he strode across and enveloped me in a big man-hug before launching into a dance with me! That's typical Ian Wright. Top man!

Wherever there is star quality there must also be stalwarts and Burnley had their fair share. Steve Davis was club captain and a rock who played his part in guiding Stan's team up to the First Division. He had two spells at the club, this was his second, and was later to become caretaker manager on a couple of occasions. Steve was a great pro and looked after himself, definitely one of the sensible ones in the crowd!

Then there was Mitchell Thomas. 'Mitch' was a helluva good professional, a defender who played a lot of games at a decent level. Stan had signed him about the time that I arrived and the defender was to see his playing days out at Turf Moor. Mitchell was instrumental in getting Ian Wright to the club. The two were big mates and larger-than-life characters. When Ian Wright joined Burnley, the two of them lived together. Life was never dull when those two were around!

Right back Dean West signed on a free transfer under the Bosman ruling. He became a fans favourite to the extent that he won about eleven of the fifteen supporters' clubs awards across the country in 2002! When I walked in to Burnley there were a few injuries and recovering injuries ready for me to deal with immediately. I sent a few to surgery, they did the rehab and Stan got them back. Midfielder Paul Weller had a major bowel operation before I went there. Nicky and I set about getting him fit again, despite Paul having much of his stomach removed. We had to be really careful with him. Overdo it and we could put him back weeks. We did a great job, even though I say it myself. Paul was to play over 250 league games up to 2004. Actually, I ended up renting a house from Paul. It was a terraced cottage in Fence, a village near Burnley, and I had it for a year. Paul gave me first option to buy when he sold up but I couldn't afford it. Looking back it would have been a nice little venture.

Characters kept the banter going in the dressing room and on the training pitch. There was plenty of laughter started by Micky Mellon, Paul Cook, Glen Little, Andy Payton and Graham Branch. They were an unbelievable set of lads and Stan was good at getting the balance right in the dressing room. The older players policed it so Stan needn't get too involved. There were some very strong characters and it doesn't surprise me that so many, like Micky, Cooky and Ronnie Jepson, went into management. In many ways Stan got the ideal group together to follow his style. There was a crazy streak running through the gaffer and plenty of it in the squad! I had a brilliant time and was the butt of much humour. I was given the nickname 'Castlemaine' . . . because I had four ex's! They were exaggerating a bit!

Paul Cook was a diamond and a genuine Scouse rascal. He was great on and off the field, inspirational and you couldn't help but like him. Paul was a man's man. He had a pub in the middle of Kirkby in Liverpool and was really one of a dying breed in the game. He has done a great job at Chesterfield. Paul knows how he wants the game to be played and how a club should be run.

This was totally opposite to the way he was at Burnley. He would have a mammoth session at his pub for the players on a Sunday so training on Mondays was hilarious as these guys tried to shake off their hangovers. Cooky and Mitchell Thomas always used to lead the running in training. They would be way out in front. Mitch wasn't a drinker as I recall, nor was Ian Wright.

In the early days before Cooky got his pub some Sundays were spent in Wakefield with Peter Swan. Peter's the funniest lad I've met in football and he loved a drink. He is a proud Yorkshireman, much like Barnsley lad Jon Parkin. They have a similar shape and build and a brilliant sense of humour! Peter and I spent a lot of time together at Burnley because he had a knee injury and there'd be many a time with Swanny where I'd be creased up with tears of laughter with his banter and antics!

The kit man at Burnley was going out with one of the girls in the office. Someone brought an old dentist's chair into the physio's room and asked if I had any use for it. Well, it stayed there. Like a lot of my generation, I took the view that I would find a use for it. I'm reluctant to throw anything away. We used to get Joe the kit man into the room and into the chair. We would shine the treatment lamp into his eyes and turn the other lights out so it was pitch black. The glare hit his face and Swanny would interrogate him about his girlfriend. Priceless.

We had a girl called Sally who would wash the kit. Swanny regularly walked in with a towel round his waist and accidentally let it drop, saying,

'What do you think of this, Sal?'

Sally would have her hand over her eyes but gaps between the fingers so she could see everything! All the time she would be giggling. Get Swanny on the pitch, though, and he was ruthless. All the strikers and centre-halves these days have pretty looks and combed hair. Swanny was one of those characters from another age who got in where it hurt and sacrificed teeth and facial features in the process.

Managers have to deal with so much. Stan was no exception. One larger-than-life Claret was striker Andy Payton. He was a local hero because he was a goal scorer. Andy was frequently in trouble with the law. Before I joined the club apparently he had assaulted someone with a baseball bat! A fella had been messing around with his girlfriend. Andy went into the guy's hairdresser's shop in Padiham and made a mess of it and him. Stan Ternent got him off with a slap on the wrist. Stan was a little intense, like Arthur Cox, but there was no doubt that he supported his players a lot. He protected them whether they were in the right or the wrong. Clubs in those days tended to be more supportive. If you had a small loan that needed repaying or a legal problem they were often there to help you out.

The locals around town knew about Andy but you never saw it in the national papers. Andy was a lad who was a target for the police. They stopped him twice for drink-driving. I came into training one Monday and Stan shouted me across, 'I don't want you to worry about the rest of the lads. I need you to go and find Andy Payton for me.'

I was one of the few who had an idea where Andy lived. I didn't know the exact house but was aware of the street. Despite his escapades, Payton kept himself to himself and had his own close group of mates. In many respects, he was an exception to the rule where footballers surround themselves with loads of mates but the lads accepted it and allowed him to get on with his life. Anyway, I knocked on a few doors and eventually found the right one. Andy's girlfriend came to door.

'Tell him it's SOSS, Stan's sent me.'

Andy came from upstairs. He'd been stopped on the way home and had run for it over hedges and fences. He had holed himself up in his girlfriend's house. Stan had told me to tell him to get into the club in the afternoon and we would go to the police with the club's solicitor. Andy knew he had no option so surrendered himself. He got away again!

The police eventually did catch up with him. He skidded on ice, hit a wall and left his car. He was spotted going into his friend's house. They found him in the wardrobe! There was a couple of years' ban and a fine for that misdemeanour. When I supervised the warm-ups in the morning at training we used to practice the Andy Payton fence jump!

Another day I went in and Stan said,

'You and I are off to Harrogate. Robbie Blake has rung in not feeling well and I don't believe him.'

Robbie was in his first of two spells at Turf Moor. A native of Middlesbrough, he had spent most of his career up to now with Bradford City. Anyway, I was quite happy to have a nice trip out for a change and Stan and I headed over the Pennines to look for Robbie! We got to his flat and it looked like he was not in. There was an open window, however, and ivy crawling up the outside of the house below it. Stan said to me,

'Climb up the ivy, SOSS, and see if he's in.'

'No way, gaffer,' was my immediate reply. 'I'm not risking serious injury.'

Stan then decided to check the local golf club. No-one had seen him there. Then it was on to several bookmakers in the locality. Same result. We ended up having a meat and potato pie, bought by Stan. That made a nice change! He was always cadging fags off me,

'Come over here, mate, and bring your fags,' he would say.

Eventually we found out that Robbie Blake had been involved in an argument with his girlfriend the night before. She had driven her car back to the north east and he had followed her. Once again, the protective side of Stan came out and he wanted to help. Robbie should have admitted he had a problem. Stan would have said, 'Family comes first'. All the good ones look at life that way. He would help in any way he could and in my time at Turf Moor there were plenty of opportunities.

Stan's caring nature often spilled over into passion and ruthlessness as he passed on his vision on how football should be played and how you should conduct yourself. Our disagreements early-doors became a thing of the past as he came to trust me. Sam Ellis said to me,

'You have to understand that we've never worked with a physio like you before'.

Stan was definitely old school. I stood up to him and we became good friends. He frequently used the phrase, 'If one of you gets cut we all bleed.' He wanted his players to stick at it through thick and thin. Stan was adamant that any opposition who kicked one of his were sorted out by his players. You are not individuals, you are a team. All the best teams display togetherness.

We played a Manchester United side which contained Paul Scholes. It was in the Worthington Cup as I recall. I had to go on three times for mistimed tackles which hurt our lads. Scholes knew what he was doing. I was laughing on the third time. The player asked why. I said,

'You've got to look after yourself. You know what he's like.'

We used to have a saying, 'retaliate first'. If he was high on you, make sure you are higher on him the next time.

Stan's volatility came out on occasions. In the away changing room at Ipswich is a big square block of wood. As far as I'm aware it's been there for years and years. It was a kicking block for when you put your boots on. It meant that you could kick your foot into the boot without damaging a door or skirting board. Stan came in once at half time, kicked the block and broke his toe!

Then there was half time at Sheffield United. There were double doors in the changing room at Bramall Lane with two wide steps down into the changing room. Directly opposite was a fire door. The lads sat by their pegs waiting for the blast to come. This was not unusual at Bramall Lane, a difficult place to get a result. Stan walks in,

'Whose bags are those?'

Players own kit bags were stacked by the fire door. Two owned up and were asked to move them. The next thing Stan's charged down the steps, crossed the changing room and kicked the fire door, kung-fu style! Stan fell in a heap on the other side of the door and there was someone there with him who had been knocked over by the force. This guy picked himself up and ran up the corridor, followed by Stan. They went out of our sight. Stan returned soon after with his tie round the side of his neck.

'See, I even fight for you lot,' he said, 'More than you do out there.' He told me to stop treating the injured players and sort him out instead! Stan had been pre-warned by Joe, Peter Reid and others about the spy on the other side of the door who listened in to half time talks from the opposition. In those times you didn't divulge anything willingly. It was like the secret service. I would be sworn to secrecy about injuries so that we didn't give opposition an advantage.

Stan had a habit of taking his players for a drink on Fridays when we went to London. We would go for a walk and he bought them all a pint.

'But I don't drink, boss.'

'You do now.'

Old mates of Stan's would regularly turn up for meals when Burnley were in the capital. Without quite being on the Oldham legendary scale we had some brilliant nights, especially when Vinny Jones was in town. Vinny had worked with Stan at Chelsea when the gaffer was assistant to Ian Porterfield in the early 1990's. He entertained us with his stories about films, hunting and poaching with his dad and friends. Vinny created this hard-man image but there was a lot more to him that he didn't want to or need to flaunt. In the 1989-90 season, he played at Leeds United, helping them gain promotion to the old First Division. Joe and I went for a chat with Leeds manager Howard Wilkinson after the game at Elland Road. Wilkinson had brought Vinny into a young side and his management style had calmed Vinny down, with just three bookings in the whole season. Joe asked Howard about Vinny,

'He's different class. He's great in the changing room and a real leader. Also, I can tell you that he does more hospital visits and charity work than anyone in the squad.'

Steve Coppell often pitched up with his many stories and dry humour but the star of them all was our old team-mate Ian Wright. He was always larger than life and arrived one day on a Harley Davidson. He lit the room up. He was that sort of person. We often stayed in the Tower Hotel, near Tower Bridge. Of all the hotels in all the towns and cities, this was my ultimate favourite stopping-off point. St Catherine's Lock was nearby with boats, bars and restaurants. There was always plenty going on.

I loved the coach trips through London from the hotel to the various grounds. It was like a free sight-seeing tour through the capital and there were different things to see each time we took the different routes to Crystal Palace, Charlton, Fulham and QPR. Once we played Palace on the Saturday and Fulham on the Tuesday. We stayed down through the weekend and Stan let the lads out on the Saturday night. Ian Wright was on hand to take a few into town while a couple of lads stumbled on a working men's club where Hugh Grant was having his birthday party!

Burnley finished seventh in the Championship in both 2000-01 and 2001-02, just outside the play-offs. Then the ITV money went and Stan called a meeting. We were in the Isle of Man at the time because we played in their tournament each pre-season. It's a beautiful island and a place where I've had a few good nights out in the past.

I particularly remember a trip with Oldham where I was talking to a girl who we nicknamed 'One Eater' because she only had one tooth. Ronnie Evans even went to get Joe Royle, telling him,

'Gaffer, you'll never believe this one SOSS is chatting to.'

Joe came across and said,

'Hi, pleased to meet you, One Eater.'

'Fucking hell,' she shouts, 'It's Joe Royle. Just wait till I tell my Dad! You're his hero!' Joe had obviously not realised that her family were massive Everton fans and was suddenly drawn in more than he wanted! Well, I was doubled over laughing!

On another evening we were mixing with some of the island's beautiful people. There was a few bob flying around and I'm chatting up this attractive lady. I go to the bar to get us a drink and get talking to Joe who says,

'You want to get in there, mate. She's from one of the richest families on the island and just been widowed.'

'Brilliant, I'm coming into money,' I thought to myself.

At breakfast the next day I'm talking to Joe, 'It could be love this. I'm really falling for her. Did you say she was from one of the richest families on the island?'

Joe replied, 'You've got it wrong, mate. That's her friend, the other one.' I had been well and truly stitched up by Joe's wicked sense of humour.

Back on the island with Burnley there was an altogether more serious situation developing as Stan had some serious things to say to the lads. Some of them wouldn't be at the club after the end of the season because ITV money for televised rights had been stopped. About sixteen players were to leave, to be replaced by nine others. Not surprisingly, we didn't do as well in the league, finishing sixteenth in 2002-03 but reaching the quarter-finals of the FA Cup. I thought that we did pretty well considering everything but Stan's contract was not renewed.

One of the players who had to take a cut when the ITV money went was Glen Little. Burnley offered him half of what he was on so he moved to Reading for fractionally more. He was awarded a new contract when Reading were promoted to the Premier League in 2006. Glen's talents as a playmaker were widely regarded as a key part of the record-breaking Championship win with 106 points. Now he must have been on at least ten to fifteen grand a week. This was basic Premier League salary. Following relegation and injuries, Glen moved through to Portsmouth, still in the Premier League, then dropped down the leagues. Recently, Paul Cook told me that he'd offered Glen the job of kitman at Chesterfield but he didn't want it.

'He's struggling,' said Cooky. 'He's spent all his money, gambled it away. There's nothing to show for all the money he had.'

Burnley's Glen Little limps off
(Picture courtesy of the 'Burnley Express')

I remember Glen on my treatment couch at Burnley. He had a brochure in his hand for a Mercedes. 'What you looking at Mercs for?' I asked him. 'You only got your BMW a few months ago.'

'I know but I'm fed up with it and fancy a change.'

'How much did you pay for your BMW?'

'Fifty grand or so. He's offered me thirty.'

I threw the book down. 'So you've lost at least twenty five grand?'

'Yes, and the Merc'll cost me sixty-five but I'm just a bit fed up and I want a new car.'

I threw the brochure on the side and thought, 'I'm not in the real world here.' It was a significant changing point in my thinking about how much top players get out of the game.

Glen was a cracking lad and a real talent but, unfortunately, he was vulnerable and it's sad to see his demise. You just don't know what might happen further down the line. His legs have gone now and he is one of many professionals who have perhaps not made the best of the money that they have earned.

Players in the higher leagues are so wealthy these days that they can buy or sell you. One of my gripes is that their wages have escalated so much whereas ours have just gone with inflation. A top Premier League physio can get a six figure annual wage, the top players easily earn that in a week. It's so different from my Oldham days when we all lived in the same area, drove similar cars and drank in the same pubs.

Paul Cook had moved down the road to Conference side Accrington Stanley and some time before the end of Stan's final season he called me. He told me that they were going full-time next season and asked if I was interested in joining them. I told him to keep me informed because I am a great believer in keeping options open. At that stage, though, Stan was still in a job and there was no sign of what was to come. Paul also had a loyalty to his former boss and didn't want to upset him because Stanley might want favours from Burnley. As soon as Stan wasn't offered a new contract at Turf Moor it opened another door for me. I was ready for a new challenge at a time when I was expanding my private business. The lower you go in the leagues, the fewer hours you tend to do and it would dovetail nicely with my private work.

Chapter Seventeen

'ACCRINGTON STANLEY? WHO ARE THEY?'

'John had the knack of taking players off the scrap heap and turning coal into diamonds.'

Everyone I spoke to thought I was stupid to move the short distance from Burnley to Accrington in 2004. It was just six or seven miles between the two clubs but there was a gulf in what they each had to offer. However, my mate Stan had left Turf Moor and I really fancied a new challenge. Accrington made no secret of their ambition to return to the Football League. They were really going to give it a go and I wanted to be a part of it. To do that the players would be going full-time. I was excited by the prospect in a similar way to a few years later when I joined Fleetwood Town.

Accrington had been in the Football League for about forty years since 1921, the original club finally folding in 1966. A revival began a couple of years later and Stanley began the long journey back. When I joined, the club was in the Conference, the top-tier of non-league football, and tantalisingly close to a famous return.

Accrington Stanley is best known to many because of an advertisement for milk which featured Liverpool legend Ian Rush. The advert was originally made in 1989 and showed two young Liverpool fans. One tried to tempt his mate to drink a glass of the healthy white stuff:

'Milk! Ugh!'

'It's what Ian Rush drinks.'

'Ian Rush?'

'Yeah. And he says that if I don't drink lots of milk when I grow up I'll end up playing for Accrington Stanley.'

'Accrington Stanley? Who are they?'

'Exactly.'

My time at Accrington Stanley was a brilliant experience. For a start I was introduced to the management style of Mr. John Coleman. I've never met anyone quite like John before or since. He told me that as a child he had read a football annual that he had got for Christmas. In it was a cartoon with a gravestone on which was written, 'Accrington Stanley RIP'. It was an image that stayed with him.

Stanley had had eight managers in a year when they signed John from Ashton United in Greater Manchester and he brought the nucleus of his side in order to establish a reliable squad.

He and assistant Jimmy Bell had a brilliant rapport with the lads and it's difficult to think of two other characters in my football lifetime who could have taken that club, with its limited resources, on the journey that they did. John and Jimmy were football guys through and through, much-travelled around the north-west and playing for clubs with minimal resources. It was a brilliant training for Accrington. They lived and breathed Accrington Stanley and gave their all. Gates were about 250 in 1999 when they took over and they increased them eight times over, a remarkable achievement when you think how many other football clubs are within an hour of the Crown Ground.

The Liverpool accent was always ringing out around the changing room and training ground. The Scouse influence was at the heart of the club. The Merseyside lads were as thick as thieves. A lot of local fans wanted local players but you couldn't knock what the Scousers did for the club and this was a major reason why John and Jimmy did such a remarkable job at Accrington. I used to tell them that they deserved medals for what they did. John had the knack of taking players off the scrap heap and turning 'coal into diamonds' as he put it.

The players weren't always getting paid and John had to tell them many times that their wages weren't coming. It might be in two or three weeks, or in dribs and drabs . . . £50 here, £100 there. How can you tell people who are working for you and busting a gut that they are not getting paid? People who, in many cases, were supporting families and had the bills to pay. John devised a system. We met in the morning for cereal, toast and a cup of tea. John would go in and start singing,

'You're not getting paid, you're not getting paid, ee-aye-addio, you're not getting paid!'

It was his way of dealing with the situation and up to a point it worked because of the strong bond within the squad. Despite the lack of resources it was a happy ship and everyone mucked in. John made the best out of adversity and used the situation to bond them together in such a way that they eventually were all singing the song about not being paid! You had to jolly them along rather than crack the whip. I didn't get paid at times and asked myself, 'Can I afford to come in?'

On one occasion I was really aggrieved that the cash wasn't forthcoming. I'd been chasing Rob Heys, the Chief Executive, who was ducking and diving out of my way. To be fair, Rob was a good guy and I had more than a degree of sympathy for him as he juggled the limited resources available to the club. I turned to John Coleman and told him that I simply couldn't afford to come in the next day.

'This isn't good enough. I can't even afford to drive in to work.'

'Why punish me?' was John's reply, 'If you do that I'm not going to have a physio. It's not my fault that you're not getting paid, it's not the lads fault.'

They were profound words and made me think I'd gone about things the wrong way. John said that he would have a word with Rob. In future I'd just have another quiet word with John and the money eventually arrived. I suppose it was part and parcel of being at a club like Stanley and there are many other lower league clubs in that position these days.

The club was full of characters fighting for the cause, none more so than Chairman Eric Whalley. Eric had played for Accrington, managed them twice, joined the board then bought the club! You can't get much more involved than that! Eric ran the operation with a strong hand. He was an old-fashioned kind of chairman who generally liked to keep his money close by but was prepared to spend when necessary. A case in point was the return of striker Paul Mullin, signed from Radcliffe Borough in 2000. After a bid of £10 000 had been rejected the previous season, Eric went back with £15 000 and got his man. It was to be a brilliant signing for the club as Paul went on to score 132 goals in over 300 games during the next decade.

Apart from his passion for football, Eric was also a keen club cricketer who had captained West Indian stars Viv Richards and Michael Holding when he played for local side Rishton in the Lancashire League. Eric tells the story that South African fast bowler Allan Donald gave a presentation once and mentioned the famous milk advert which he had remembered seeing in South Africa!

The lack of money was reflected in the facilities. There was no first aid room as such. It was really a store room and I had to clear the rubbish off the beds before I could use them. The room had a big steel door with a red cross on it. There was a two inch gap under the door and the wind whistled in. There was no rehab equipment. You were limited in what you could do with the lads and rarely were we able to train on the pitch. Despite these restrictions, I did at least have an assistant! Craig Yuill eventually went to Manchester City then I got my friend Ronnie Evans in.

We had to beg, steal and borrow facilities to complement the lack of them at the ground. We usually finished up training at council-owned playing fields with dark, dingy changing areas that were never cleaned out. The shower areas were often horrible. I would set up a portable bed in the changing rooms there. In fact I got very used to carrying my bed around with me. Ronnie did Monday to Friday and took the reserves midweek. We worked on split sites so it was good to have two bodies—one at training, the other dealing with rehab.

Wilson's Playing Fields was made up of three or four football pitches with a running track and a cricket pitch in the middle. The rain always produced a massive puddle of water. More a lake in fact! When it was like that the lads would try some running, then hope for 5-a-side on a decent area after which they stripped off down to shorts and dived head-first through the water. They all ran at it together and it was spectacular to watch! I have to say that there was always extra pressure on in dodgy weather conditions. With a small squad, you were limited as to how you could train the team. It became more risky in terms of injuries. The playing fields had a room used by the ground maintenance lads. It was attached to the changing complex. It was nicely done out with a laminate floor, kitchen, tables and chairs. We regularly popped in for tea and toast with the park keepers and had a really good laugh with them. I have to say that the lads were magnificent throughout my time there, coping with everything that was thrown at them.

One year we were able to use the Rolls Royce facilities at Barnoldswick. I had a decent room I could use and there was a gym there as well. If it rained we were never able to get on pitches so John and Jimmy took the lads on a canal run. Sometimes they would turn to the lads and say,

'Anyone who swims across the canal and back can get changed and go home.'

Andy Mangan and Ian Craney were usually the two who took up the challenge. They were both big characters who liked to be at the centre of things. They half-swam, half-waded across the murky water of the Leeds-Liverpool Canal, much to the delight of the rest. They would then return bedraggled along the half mile or so to the changing rooms.

They got fed, then played the snooker tables in the social club. Mangy's bravado backfired on him on one occasion when he ended up with a rash all over his body and had to go straight to the doctor! You can imagine the stick he took for that!

We eventually made an agreement with Hyndburn Leisure Centre to use their facilities. They were much better and going indoors was smashing, particularly in the middle of winter when the weather was really bad. The staff put classes on for the players. They usually did a mixture of pilates, yoga and core work. There was also Body Pump, which involved exercises to music with weights and that was hard. There were also chances to play badminton, five-a-side and basketball. The arrangement eventually came to an end because Chairman Eric Whalley refused to pay for the extra classes that the girls did. Hyndburn Council had allowed Eric to use Clayton and Hyndburn for a nominal fee but the girls' sessions had been extra. There was a bit of a fall-out and we moved on to another facility.

I rented a room in a private gym in a hotel near Accrington. I had a bit of an argument with Eric over it. I paid rent and saw a few private patients there as well as treating the players and using the gym there for them. Eric wanted a share of the private clinic. I told him there wasn't anything to share. I was paying £50 a week for the room and treated his players there. I thought if I could get a couple of private patients a week I'd cover it. I didn't think for one moment about making a profit. Anyway Eric didn't like it. He forbade me from continuing and we had a bit of an argument over it.

Despite our disagreement on that occasion I have to say that Eric Whalley was brilliant for Accrington. Without him we wouldn't have got into the Football League. At a cash-strapped club he made sure everyone got paid what they were owed but just couldn't guarantee to always do it on time. He was always honest and up front about this which was better than a person avoiding phone calls, coming up with untruths and false promises.

A couple of times a season, when facilities were a struggle or the lads were looking jaded, John and Jimmy would bring them in and say,

'Right, a tenner a man and you can go home without training.'

The deal was that everyone had to pay. Some didn't have money, others only a fiver. They would go into a big huddle and have a whip round. One or two were adamant that they wouldn't pay but, on the whole, it worked. The players got the money back through a fund which supported activities like go-karting and paintballing. There were regular golf days as well. It all added to team spirit. The coach returning from away games was nicknamed the 'party bus'. It's so important to mix things up a bit when you are in and out of each other's pockets and John Coleman and Jimmy Bell were masters at it.

Accrington had their first bit of luck for forty years when local lad Brett Ormerod impressed Blackpool to the extent that they were prepared to pay £50 000 for the striker in 1997. The story did not end there because a sell-on clause in his contract meant that a subsequent million pound plus move to Southampton in 2001 netted the club a further £250 000 because of an agreement that Accrington would receive a 25% sell-on clause. Having amassed the money the club decided to give it a go and push for a regaining of their league status. They invested in players rather than the infrastructure. Winning the Northern Premier League in 2002-03 followed quickly after the club had been paid the cash. Further funds came from an FA Cup run in 2003-04 when the team got as far as the Third Round.

After finishing tenth in the Conference in two successive seasons, promotion back into the Football League was achieved in my second year at the Crown Ground. We took the Conference by storm. There was a defining moment which remains as clear as glass in my mind, the day we signed a new goalkeeper. We played Altrincham away after a poor start in the first few games of the season. We had this keeper who was the wrong side of thirty. He had had a decent league career and appeared a good signing. Up front was target man Paul Mullin who was six feet odd and vital to our hopes of success. Mullin would stand wide right or left from goal kicks and we played off him. Anyway, at Altrincham he went wide right. Our keeper saw him and hooked it wide left. Mullin went left and the keeper sliced it right. He just couldn't find

Paul at all that afternoon. John came in at half time and threw a plate of Jaffa Cakes at the keeper, which he dropped!

'Fucking hit him,' John ordered and gave his keeper a right dressing down. We got beat. The next day the keeper told us he was quitting. He had a serious ankle injury the season before and had spent a lot of time at Lilleshall so decided to retire.

We were left without a keeper so John got this lad Darren Randolph on loan from Charlton. He was only a young pro at the time but eventually made it into the Scottish Premier League. His party piece was to catch the ball one-handed off people's heads. More importantly, he pinpointed Mullin every time. We started winning games and we built from Paul's distribution. Ian Craney and Anthony Barry took the ball off him and we played in their half which John liked. It was a season-shaping point. All was going well at Christmas when Jimmy told me that we only had our new keeper for three months. However, he had been told by Darren that Charlton would send the other one who 'was nearly as good'. His name was Rob Elliot. Rob arrived and the momentum continued.

We played Exeter away in February, a long, long way involving a stay over. The game was live on Sky and Exeter had high expectations. We battered them. Peter Cavanagh cut one of their lads in two early doors. How he stayed on the pitch, heaven only knows. He wouldn't have these days. That tackle, which you can still see on 'You Tube,' set the precedent and we ran them ragged. On the way home the lads were chanting, 'We've won the league'. It was Anthony Barry's last game. Ant was one of Accrington's Liverpool-born contingent and a top man, the heartbeat of the club. I was to see a lot of him again at Fleetwood, too much regrettably because he was to suffer a career-threatening injury and we spent many hours together. Happily, Anthony recovered and is playing at Forest Green.

Romuald 'Romy' Boco, Ian Craney, Gary Roberts and Paul Mullin won us promotion at Accrington because they scored the goals. Guys like that were capable of taking an ordinary game by the scruff of the neck and transforming it with a quality strike. An Ian Craney goal at Rotherham is a typical example which sticks clearly in my mind. I remember 'Romy' signing from French side Chamois Niortais in 2005 and he quickly became a fans favourite. He came from nowhere to make a fantastic impact at the Crown Ground. We got him just before the transfer deadline and Romy was soon well on the way to legendary status when he scored Stanley's first two Football League goals, in a 2-1 win over Barnet. Gary Roberts was special. We picked him up from Welshpool Town in 2005 and Gary was one of three signings that the club made at the time. With that background he kind of snuck in under the radar and not too many people stood up and took notice. He quickly grew in stature. One move underlined his quality. We played Torquay away. Gary chased the ball to the right corner flag. Their centre half tracked him. Gary nonchalantly flicked the ball over his head and fired a volley into the top corner. I thought at that moment, 'He's not going to be with us much longer'. Sure enough, Gary went to Ipswich Town and is still going strong in League football.

A nineteen-game unbeaten run from October to March had set us up to succeed and the club returned to the Football League in 2006. I was privileged to be involved in a historic occasion as Accrington returned to the big-time. It was a modern-day fairy tale.

Winning the league was a bitter-sweet experience for Peter Cavanagh. Leading the lads to the title was a career highlight put into perspective by the tragic death of his brother Tony after an attack in Liverpool city centre. The incident served to bring a close-knit group of lads even closer and I remember a match at Grays Athletic down in Essex where they all wore special t-shirts in support of Cav. We were battling with Grays at the top of the league at the time, went there and won. Grays were one of a number of teams who had thrown money into the playing staff to make an effort for promotion. There were many places we went where you'd look around and think, 'We won't win here.' But we did. We were so often seen as the underdogs and John Coleman liked it that way.

You cannot underestimate the achievement of getting back after forty-four years in the wilderness. The Conference has any number of former league clubs in its ranks. Many clubs with long League histories, such as Stockport County and Grimsby Town, have dropped out and failed to get back.

I wasn't under contract at Accrington but I don't think that John Coleman was best-pleased when I accepted a new job. My old mate from Burnley, Stan Ternent, was now at League One Huddersfield Town and he rang me to see if I was interested in moving across the Pennines in the summer of 2008. He had replaced former Oldham legend Andy Ritchie in April of that year on a three-year contract. Ex-Town player, Ronnie Jepson, became his assistant at the same time. Ronnie, like me, was someone who Stan knew well and could trust.

The end at Accrington was really down to me. I had spent four years in limited surroundings. I still took a mobile bed backwards and forwards. We had returned to the Football League, an amazing achievement, but my situation hadn't changed. I felt that there was very little else I could achieve there and that there was no mental challenge left. I could have spent all day massaging people's legs. It was a lazy man's way of warming-up. I used to say to the lads,

'Good players don't need a massage, bad ones aren't worth it.'

They'd scratch their heads and walk away. Players always asked me for a massage. I'd ask why and they'd maybe say it was a hamstring problem. I told them to get on with it and if it was still hurting after training to come back. Nine out of ten didn't. I had injured players to treat and you couldn't forever be massaging. They might take twenty minutes, half an hour each. Then you'd get five coming in at ten, half an hour before training started.

Huddersfield Town presented a whole new challenge with a set-up far superior to the Crown Ground at Accrington. There was a treatment room and gym at the training ground and treatment room, gym and pool at the stadium. For me it was a no brainer. I had come to a standstill and now I could go and do some proper work. I was excited about the move and working with Stan again but, looking back, the bubble was to burst all too soon.

Chapter Eighteen

A BRIEF VISIT TO YORKSHIRE

'Everything was set-up for an exciting new venture.'

There was absolutely no comparison between the facilities available at Accrington and Huddersfield. A decision had been made in August 1992 to build a new stadium for Huddersfield Town. Construction began the following year and the job was completed in time for the 1994-95 season. For the first ten years or so, the stadium was known as the Alfred McAlpine Stadium, then it became the Galpharm and the John Smith's as sponsorship deals changed. The ground is shared by the town's football and rugby league sides. I was joining a club with facilities, tradition, infrastructure and support. What could be better? Stan clearly wanted me and I moved to Yorkshire on a three-year contract, full of hope and excitement.

Backed by a large budget, Stan signed eleven new players including ex-Accrington favourite Gary Roberts and a former player of his, Chris Lucketti, who moved from Sheffield United and was immediately made club captain. It was a much-changed team who took to the pitch at the start of the 2008-09 season. Things quickly went pear-shaped. We hit a rocky spell early on in the season with just four wins in fifteen league matches and there was some unrest in a team that contained a number of strong characters. Things were made worse by Stan's wish to wage war with Director of Football Development, Gerry Murphy. Following the termination of Andy Ritchie's contract, Murphy had been put in temporary charge of the first team for the second time. This period included the last home game of the season, against Walsall, and the last away match, at Luton Town. As Director, Gerry was technically above the manager and he had some very strong allies in the club. Stan was not the sort of guy to sit back and be steam-rollered. He was determined to clip Gerry's wings. Stan wanted to seize power back and it became a goal that side-tracked him from his main purpose as manager of the club. Unfortunately, the battle he started affected his running of the club and Stan spent as much time thinking about Gerry as the football.

One of Gerry's roles was to run the academy. When he was made caretaker manager he used to bring his young players in from the academy. Results improved short term but the kids couldn't sustain it. Gerry would often keep the best training pitches for his academy sides. On that issue Stan was adamant.

'We have the best pitches for the first team. The first team is the main team and without it everything else fails'.

In November I was to experience one of those days I will never forget. Stan arrived late for training one Monday. He pulled us all into his office and said,

'I've just told the Chairman. It's me or him. One of us has to go.'

I looked at Ronnie Jepson and coach Mick Docherty who were both gently shaking their heads. Stan went out. I said to the others,

'It won't affect us, will it?'

They replied, 'It will.'

It was a battle that Stan didn't win and he left after six months in charge. Had he not given the ultimatum to the Chairman we might have kept our jobs a bit longer. If results on the pitch had been better the outcome could have been different. Stan could have argued from a position of strength.

The next day Stan was not there and Mick and Ronnie had disappeared as well. It was a classic case of a manager's actions bringing down those around him. Instead, Gerry Murphy was there organising.

'The Chairman wants to see you at the ground,' he told me with a hint of a smile on his face.

In my mind I started thinking how much compensation I could get. I had been at Huddersfield for about six months and, as with Oldham, November was not a good time to be cast out. I rehearsed my lines,

'Ok, you don't want me anymore. Whatever I say or do won't change your mind on that. You've made your decision etc.'

An accident on the road ahead of me prevented me getting through to the ground so the Chairman came to me twenty-four hours later.

'I've given it a lot of thought,' he said. 'I want a clean sweep to get rid of all Stan's men. You've not done anything wrong.'

I brought up the subject of compensation. After all, I had signed a three-year contract. Unfortunately, the terms of my contract didn't give me any rights until after six months had been completed. I was just short. The club gave me three months money. I wanted six and would have definitely got it after six months work.

Not many jobs come up mid-season so you're then into a waiting game. Six months would have been fairer because I could have bided my time and taken stock ahead of a new start next season. I wasn't given that opportunity and, instead, had to make three months money last six. Huddersfield sacked me on November 5th . . . . and my youngest lad, Alfie, was born on 22nd November. There was no remorse and they tried to deny me every penny they could.

Fortunately, I had my private work to fall back on and increased the hours. It made me think how important it was to keep the private stuff going, my bread and butter should the fickle world of football let me down. Over eighteen years or so I had built up a good client base. The all-singing, all-dancing opportunity at Huddersfield had not lasted long. I was so upset after leaving that I decided I would never go back into the Football League again because of the way it had affected me and my family.

I spoke to Stan a long time after. He said that the Murphy issue had affected his home life. He couldn't get to sleep at night and his relationship with his wife had suffered. He had talked it through with his missus who was right behind his decision to approach the Chairman with the ultimatum.

I have got many friends in the game at all levels and one of them contacted me in my hour of need. Neil Tolson was manager of Hyde United, one of the top non-league sides in the Manchester area. Neil was a good striker at lower league level who I had come across as a young lad at Oldham. He had joined Hyde as a player back in 2003 and was combining the roles of player and manager, having taken over as gaffer after the club's poor start to the Conference North 2008-09 season. Hyde's physio was leaving in January 2009 to take up a full-time post and he offered me the chance to take over. My private practice would be unaffected, the club was only just up the road from home and I was working for someone I knew. It was an arrangement that suited me and it further made my mind up that I would not to go back into full-time football.

Despite the advantages surrounding my new job, the coming months were to prove challenging on and off the pitch. Results left us twentieth in the league and facing relegation only to get a reprieve as King's Lynn's stadium did not meet league standards. Hyde were undergoing serious financial problems and on 24th September 2009, the club was officially wound-up in the High Court with tax debts of around £120 000. Sufficient funds were raised over the next few days, including a bucket collection at Manchester City, to lodge an appeal and the decision was reversed on 30th September. They were very difficult times but we all mucked in together and it was good from that point of view. There was a brilliant set of lads and I enjoyed myself, revelling in the role that Neil had given me. It was a three-man band with the two of us alongside former Burnley midfielder Gerry Harrison who was both player and assistant-manager. I was brought in on discussions about players, took warm-ups and got involved in training. I have to say that the relegation pressure was not nice, though, despite our reprieve. It was the third relegation scrap of my career, having already gone down with Oldham and Stoke. Thankfully I've been involved in more promotions than relegations.

We got a couple of players in after the winding-up order was reversed and things looked a bit healthier. Pre-season was good. Our second game of the new season took us to Fleetwood Town. Neil and Gerry had a touchline ban at the time so I was on my own at Highbury Stadium. At the end of the game, Fleetwood manager Micky Mellon pulled me over and said,

'We're going full-time, SOSS. My physio can't commit so how are you fixed?'

I had known Micky from both Blackpool and Burnley days and he sold it to me that Fleetwood were going places. It sounded a similar challenge to that presented by Accrington Stanley. Any thoughts of never going back to full-time and into the Football League disappeared out of the window. I told Micky that I was definitely interested in what he had to say.

I put it to the back of my mind and carried on with my duties for Hyde. After a game in October I was pulling up on my drive when Micky rang me,

'We've got a vacancy for a physio. How are you fixed, mate?'

'Now? 'Yes, I'll do it.' I never even blinked. I rang Neil Tolson who thankfully understood, although I'm not sure that the Hyde committee did. I was on my way back into full-time employment a few short months after vowing never to. The destination was one of the most ambitious clubs in the north-west and the prospect stirred something inside me.

Chapter Nineteen

LIFE WITH THE COD ARMY

'In my mind we were far and away the best team'

Fleetwood Town had been making rapid progress up the non-league pyramid. Chairman, Andy Pilley, certainly had the money to invest in football but he was also a knowledgeable and enthusiastic fan of the game, unlike some Chairmen that I've met. He had joined the club in 2003 and set about transforming it both physically and in its mind-set. He tells a story about when he first looked round the dilapidated stadium. He tried to open a window and it fell out! It was that sort of place back then.

I remember an early example of how things could well be different at Fleetwood from other clubs at this level. When Hyde had played at Highbury on the day that Micky first spoke to me about a job, Steve McNulty was in the stands. Steve had been the club's record signing when he moved from Barrow at the start of the season. His problem was that he was carrying too much weight and Micky was not playing him. It made the Hyde lads laugh that they'd paid top wages for him yet could afford to have him sitting in the stands! Steve got his head down, trained hard and emerged as a commanding centre-half who was the leader that the club needed on and off the field.

I knew the area, of course, after my times at Blackpool and soon settled in to life among the Cod Army. I was to enjoy a fantastic three years at Fleetwood and experience some of those special qualities about a football club that I had not enjoyed since my Oldham days.

I joined a management team who interacted perfectly. Alongside Micky was assistant manager Craig Madden. Craig had been a prolific goalscorer in his time, particularly at Bury. Steve Macauley combined work as a coach with a physiotherapy job in the NHS. Steve was a former player at Fleetwood but had made his name at Crewe Alexander and was highly respected around Highbury having performed a number of roles for the club over many years. Danny Moore combined physio work with looking after the kit as well as sorting the many arrangements needed to get the team from A to B and back again. Having three of us with physiotherapy experience was a nice situation to be in although Steve concentrated mainly on his coaching work.

The treatment room was round the back of the Highbury Stand which ran down one side of the pitch. It was big enough for two beds. Training was at Collins Park in south Blackpool on the way out to Lytham and St. Anne's. The facilities weren't on a par with some clubs I'd been at but I could tell from the start that I was going to enjoy life at Fleetwood Town.

The team's first priority was to get out of Conference North, one level below the Conference itself. That was far from straightforward as we battled for the automatic promotion spot with neighbours and rivals Southport. The situation was complicated by the Farsley Celtic issue. Farsley played near Leeds with a history going back a hundred years. Unpaid taxes began to grow and the club reportedly owed up to three quarters of a million pounds. One thing led to another and Farsley was eventually disbanded in March 2010. Their playing record that season was wiped out meaning that Fleetwood Town were deprived of the points gained from two league victories while midfield player Jamie Milligan saw a remarkable goal from his own half wiped out of the record books. Milly had spotted the Farsley keeper off his line and did him. He had a unique talent but, sadly, a unique knee problem as well. It was a relic from a previous injury some years ago. A piece of bone wore away and they had to drill the area hoping that scar tissue would replace the bone. Milly worked hard on his strength and got back on to the pitch. He had an unbelievable left foot and vision to match. He was also one of the most lethal dead-ball specialists I think I've seen.

The decision to take the points from matches against Farsley Celtic kicked things off between Fleetwood and Southport as it favoured Southport enough to give them advantage at the top of the league. They lost fewer points out of it and Fleetwood's complaints went all the way to FA Headquarters at Wembley. Nothing was changed and Town faced the play-offs. There were many out there looking for us to fail. A lot of jealousy and anger had crept in because of Andy Pilley's ability to attract top players on good wages.

The play-offs paired us with Manchester side Droylsden with the first leg at their place. We played lamely and came away 2-0 down. Having held a high-scoring team for seventy minutes we conceded twice in quick succession. Fleetwood was not my first experience of play-offs but the previous two had been losing ones, at Oldham and Stoke. It looked like I was going to experience an unwelcome hat-trick. We got on the coach after the game thinking we had blown it. It was a real wake-up call and on the way back we knew that we had to be on our best form to get anything from the second leg.

There was plenty of drama to come as the lads put in a much-improved performance in the return. Micky worked on them and they were tremendous back at Highbury. Our side was packed with good footballers as well as our 'dogs of war'. Micky used to say,

'Should we release the dogs of war?'

I would nod my head and say, 'Let's do it'.

Out would come Jamie McGuire and Steve Connors, two ultra-competitive midfielders who never took a step backwards. Jamie was a chip off the old block, Reggie's lad in every way. He was a constant reminder of my teaching times on the Wirral where Reggie shared that crafty cigarette with me on the top deck of the games bus.

As I said, the lads really stepped it up, determined to get out of a division where they considered themselves not only to be the best side but also unjustly penalised with the Farsley situation. We had wiped out the deficit by half time and all looked good in front of a huge crowd. The match went to extra time and centre-back Simon Grand's first goal for Town put us in the driving seat only for us to concede seven minutes from full-time. My God, it was getting tense! Penalties followed, in front of our own supporters in the packed Memorial Stand. The shoot-out was all-square with one kick left. Nick Rogan drove Fleetwood's penalty into the roof of the net and then keeper Danny Hurst saved to his left. The Highbury pitch disappeared as the fans invaded it!

We had home advantage for a one-leg final and there were some fiery comments heating things up before the game with Alfreton Town. A prominent Conference North manager showed clearly that he wanted Alfreton to win and hoped that Fleetwood would get a good beating.

Comments like this can work in your favour but I have to say the mood in the camp was restrained. Micky appeared quite calm on the exterior. Over three and a half thousand packed into Highbury and saw Fleetwood take an early lead through Gareth Seddon although I think Nathan Pond is still claiming it! Alfreton struggled to break us down but were right back in the game with ten minutes left when Andy Todd was fouled in the box. Danny couldn't repeat his heroics of the semi-final as Todd put the spot kick past him. Just two minutes later veteran striker Lee Thorpe struck the winner from close range and we were promoted!

Winning the final was great for two reasons. Not only were we joining the Conference for the first time but we were also going full-time. Whether we had stayed in the Conference North or gone up to the Conference that was going to happen. It was a brilliant situation for a team at that level to be in. Knowing that we would go full-time whatever the outcome was a big motivational factor. The jealousy created by others on the circuit just made us focus more and we were now able to transform our players' lives. No longer did they have to juggle work and football.

In my mind we were far and away the best team in the division that season and deserved to go up. I had so wanted to get out of Conference North. I was very driven and intense from the moment I listened to Micky's desire to aim for the Football League. I put pressure on myself to achieve it. The Farsley situation had made it more difficult but losing the points was a setback which Micky channelled into something positive.

I had known Micky Mellon for many years as a player which made our relationship different from those with other managers where you are getting to know each other for the first time. Micky transferred his skills brilliantly to management. He picked up on things that were not working on the pitch or in training and he wasn't scared to put things right. I was impressed with how he organised and got his message over to the players. He could tear a strip off them if the situation demanded but was always on hand to give considered and constructive advice. Micky always kept me in the loop. I never forced my feelings on him but if asked I gave opinions and suggestions. He knew that I had a lot of experience in football at that stage and that I had sampled life in the lower leagues with Altrincham and Accrington Stanley. Micky took his staff's thoughts seriously so we were all in it together but eventually it was his decision that counted and that is what makes a good manager. Micky was also very supportive of the family ethic. All the best managers looked after the players and their staff. Micky understood and sympathised when problems occurred away from the game.

We went into the Conference on a high after a pre-season in Austria which opened one or two eyes. At the complex we met representatives from Football League clubs asking who we were, what league we were in and how we could afford such a facility. It was a brilliant centre, no distractions for the players but a little bar by the lake which the staff cycled to after work!

At training camp in Austria (Picture courtesy of Derick Thomas, Fleetwood Town Football Club)

Everyone was motivated knowing that they had a wonderful opportunity ahead of them. The Conference North days were over, the slate was wiped clean and it was time to perform at the top table of non-league football.

We started with a draw at Rushden and Diamonds, a late goal from a corner depriving us of all three points. A promising start was followed by a sticky spell in mid-season but the lads came through well to go through nine unbeaten games and make the play-offs for a second successive season. Having lost 2-0 at home to AFC Wimbledon, we travelled south for one of the worst games I have ever experienced. Before the match the talk was that if we got a goal back quickly we were back in the game. Nerves would begin to spread around the Wimbledon supporters and players. Well, we had hardly sat down in the dug-out when they took the lead! I think it was Craig Madden who threw his notebook down and we had to sit and endure ninety minutes of torture with the Wimbledon fans crowded around the dug-out. We kept looking at the ground for a hole to jump into. You sit through the good times and have to also face up to the bad and that was one bad ninety minutes. For the record, we lost 8-1 on aggregate so you'll be able to work out the damage done that night!

Wimbledon had been a bridge too far. However, the experience that night and throughout the season had shown us what was required. Fitness levels were undoubtedly higher and another big difference was that travelling was more intense than in the Conference North, where most of the games were northern-based. Now we faced a glut of southern games with the necessary overnight stays. We played Histon on a cold, foggy and grim Tuesday night in Cambridge. I think we lost 1-0. The game had been within an ace of being called off and we had a long journey back.

Not for the first time, Micky channelled disappointment and turned it into a positive. Following the Wimbledon disaster he worked on improving the team and raising fitness levels was a priority as he upped the training regime. We had a mixed start to the 2011-12 season, the low point being a 4-0 drubbing at Barrow. By the start of the next game just three days later, Jamie Vardy had arrived at Highbury. I remember Jamie coming into Micky's office. Micky said,

'You ok?'

Vards said, 'Yes, fine gaffer.'

'. . . ok you are playing then.'

Simple as that. The lad from Sheffield had never played at this level before and was immediately catapulted into the team for the visit of York City. It was a surprising selection choice so soon but it didn't bother Jamie one bit and he walked out of Micky's office to get on with it. I could tell immediately that there was a spring in his step and a real swagger. Jamie showed some good touches in a goalless draw and I saw one or two things which looked promising. There was excitement around Highbury as a number of clubs had been after the FC Halifax striker's signature but little did we know quite what his impact would prove to be. I've worked with far better footballers than Jamie Vardy will ever be but, apart from Kevin Keegan's impact on

Tyneside, I've not seen any transform a club's fortunes in quite the way Vards did. Make no mistake, he wasn't the only threat we had but he was the catalyst on many occasion . . . passionate, unpredictable and inspirational. He could win games single-handedly just as the great players I've worked with could and he did it by taking the situation by the scruff of the neck.

Jamie Vardy, Fleetwood Town's inspirational striker
(Picture courtesy of Derick Thomas, FTFC)

Vardy's next five games featured five goals and a sending-off! Things were never quiet when he was around! He served his suspension and returned to the team on 11th October for a home game against lowly Newport County. It was a match that had three points written all over it, particularly after Gareth Seddon scored in the first couple of minutes. Things went from bad to worse, Sedds saw a red card and Newport triumphed 4-1. The Cod Army were stunned, we all were. That was a significant match because, from that dismal Tuesday night we set off on a 29-match unbeaten run. We played some brilliant football, particularly away from home, and bagged 76 goals. Vardy's share was

26. Goals win you games and this breeds confidence in the other players. Suddenly you become a good team. It was a pleasure to watch.

Looking back, the arrival of Jamie Vardy will be remembered by many as the main reason behind Fleetwood Town's promotion to the Football League. Without him we would have gone into the lottery of the play-offs. Jamie would also be the first to admit that he had lots of good players around him, not least Peter Cavanagh. Having been at Accrington Stanley with Cav I was instrumental in getting him, Ian Craney and Anthony Barry, all former Stanley players, to Fleetwood. I'd sounded them out as to what they were doing and felt responsible for them making a success of the move. I also knew Andy Mangan from Accy days. Micky told me that we were after Andy and I said it would be a good move but didn't get involved beyond that.

Cav had been a leader and an inspiration for Accrington, a popular lad at the heart of the club. As time passed at Fleetwood, Micky was repeatedly worried that he was not going anywhere. He took a lot of flack over the lad and used to say to me,

'Cav's causing me problems, mate. There's people getting on his back and wondering why he's not doing the business.'

Despite all the coaching and monitoring it just wasn't working out. There were murmurings among the supporters and Cav couldn't dislodge the consistent Shaun Beeley from the right full back position. Injuries had once again affected him, as they had previously in his career. He had regular knee and ankle problems. I felt more and more strongly that I was to blame for him not making the grade at Fleetwood. Micky had even got to the point where he thought that Cav should find another club. There wasn't anything nasty or ruthless about it. You win some, you lose some and this arrangement hadn't worked.

We had won five on the bounce after the Newport defeat and suddenly there was an injury issue in midfield. Cav had played there in his youth before converting to full back and stepped into the side for his first game of the season, midweek at Gateshead. A couple of games later he was back in for the FA Cup match at Yeovil. We had held the League

One side 2-2 at Highbury and Cav came in for the replay. By default he went in as a stop-gap and, suddenly, we had found the missing link. Cav's sheer determination shone through and he was rejuvenated. He had lost pace at full back but in midfield he linked everything up, kept things simple and put his foot in. Cav organised, rolled a ball and shone. We won that night and very soon Peter Cavanagh became the first name on the team sheet and a key part of our success over the rest of the season. I was delighted for him. His performances strengthened the spine that is so important in all sides and we had it at Fleetwood from Scott Davies in goal through Steve McNulty in defence, Jamie McGuire and Peter Cavanagh in midfield to Jamie Vardy and Andy Mangan up front.

As the unbeaten run went past Christmas and into the New Year I started getting a feeling that it was meant to be. We could go up. We were a quality side and had taken the Conference by storm in just our second season. My desire to get back into the Football League matched that of Micky and the Chairman's. It wasn't St. James' Park in front of massive crowds or Boundary Park in the Premier League but what I experienced during this time at Highbury were some of my most exciting times in the game. Micky and I shared a desire to be back in the club of 92, members of the Football League. It became a motivation for each of us to deliver to the other. Match by match it was becoming a reality. In the end, we crossed the line without even playing! We had drawn at home to Lincoln City on Friday 13th April. It was a televised match and everything was geared up for a massive celebration. The television company had its fingers crossed! We did everything but score the winner. It was just one of those nights. The next day, Wrexham failed to get the result they needed and we were up into the Football League for the first time in the club's history. I suppose a lot of Fleetwood people will remember where they were when Town went up. The Chairman was at a zoo down south with his family. I had been watching the results come in on the television and wanted to speak to someone when I knew we were up but everyone's phones had gone mad!

A home defeat against Luton Town on the last day was hardly the way to finish. We would like to have gone out in style and there were some

Conference records that could have been beaten but the lads had done the business. That's all that mattered. Micky wasn't happy, though. He had wanted to forge ahead to the very end and show people that we were worthy winners. It was a bit of a downer at the death but we got the open-topped ride and the Civic functions!

Chapter Twenty

THE CLUB OF 92

'It's like the land of the giants out there, gaffer.'

After a good summer break with no play-offs to go through, we prepared for what would be a massive step-up into the Football League and had to do so without Jamie Vardy who moved on to Championship side Leicester City after a host of clubs wanted his signature. At a reported transfer fee of a million pounds it had been a good bit of business for the club but we would miss him. After a slow start he has begun to prove himself at the higher level and was a key part of the squad who regained their Premier League status in 2014. I am delighted for him.

One big difference between league and non-league is the physical size of players. There are definitely some teams whose main priority is to stay in the league and where entertainment is secondary but then there are the power teams like Gillingham, Port Vale, Rotherham and Bradford who all went up in our first season. These games were full-throttle. It was proper, high-octane stuff. Warfare! I used to see them going out to warm up and I'd go back into Micky and tell him, 'It's like the land of the giants out there, gaffer.'

It was quite an opening to our League career. Qualification for the Capital One Cup brought Nottingham Forest to Highbury in the First

Round on the Monday before the season started. Then it was Torquay at home followed by Bradford City and Burton Albion away in the first week. The match at Bradford was a ferocious, powerful game. There was tension on the pitch and the game was played at a fast pace in front of a passionate crowd of nearly ten thousand. It brought back memories of being on the end of some beatings at Valley Parade when I was at Oldham. I thought that Fleetwood deserved to win on the night but in the end there was just one goal in it and it went to Bradford.

The first win and the first goal came at Burton Albion, starting a run of four successive victories and things were settling in well in the top six. Morecambe away on a beautiful day in early September was brilliant, a Jon Parkin hat trick silencing the Shrimps supporters in a 4-0 victory. The big man had been getting the sort of stick that easily came his way from opposition fans but silenced them by cupping his hand to his ear as if to say, 'You've gone quiet!' Jon was typical of the type of player we were able to attract as we moved forward. He brought a mass of experience gained from clubs like Hull City and Preston North End.

Celebrating a last minute win over Northampton Town with Fleetwood Town's Jamie McGuire (Picture courtesy of Derick Thomas, FTFC)

League clubs came and went and we held our own on most occasions. Lessons were learned, not least when Port Vale pasted us 5-2 at Highbury. We had a run of one win in seven through October and November. There were five draws in that time and home form was suddenly hit-and-miss. In fact, we had tended to play better away from Highbury in my time at Fleetwood. The size of the pitch doesn't help. The width we use is a bare minimum so there is less space between defenders and less room to work in. Struggling managers prefer more compact pitches because they can close things down and this happened on many occasions through the Conference North, Conference and into the Football League. Teams would set their stall out at Highbury and invite us to break them down. They were well-organised and I took my hat off to them.

Micky went for a 4-5-1/4-3-3 flexible formation at home. This is usually more familiar on away grounds but that was his shape with the players he had. Parkin was effective when fit and he soon had two hat tricks to his name. A lot of the spade work fell on David Ball's shoulders and he needed a mobile physical presence alongside him. There wasn't another striker. Andy Mangan was injured and it just didn't happen for Steven Gillespie. There is a player inside Steve and he had been successful elsewhere but he was struggling for form at this time. I got the impression that the Chairman wanted two strikers at home.

Bit by bit, the operation began to fracture and I was entering a difficult time both personally and professionally. My mother was ill and she died on 20th November 2012, the Tuesday before our game at Dagenham and Redbridge. I missed the home defeat to neighbours Accrington Stanley and was given the rest of the week off before joining the team coach at Junction 19 on the M6 for the journey south to East London. This was to be the first of three long and arduous trips with the team. When I stepped on board at the Windmill pub I got the feeling that the atmosphere around the management table on the coach was low-key. Normally it would be bubbling and the banter would flow. There would be warm welcomes from Micky, Craig, Steve and Danny but not on this occasion. Micky quietly revealed to me the details of an argument he had had with the Chairman. He asked me for my opinion on what he had done and I gave him it.

To be honest, the news deflated me. On the back of the issues with my mother this was not a good development. Suddenly, a long journey felt so much longer. I spent much of it thinking about what the future might have in store. I thought back to the fall-out at Huddersfield when Stan Ternent had taken Gerry Murphy on. It had affected me so much that I had vowed never to return to full-time football. To deepen the mood, the weather was foul. We spent the night in the south-east before heading for Dagenham's East End ground. They beat us in the most unfortunate circumstances. Driving rain had made play difficult and they won with a late, late penalty which we should never have conceded. Our centre-back suffered a broken toe and a five-hour journey back was made worse by the television not working on the bus! I sat on my own with countless thoughts again rushing through my mind. I used to enjoy travelling so much. It was all part and parcel of what I loved about football. It had suddenly become hard work and the Dagenham and Redbridge nightmare was to be followed by two other long away-days which almost finished me off.

The defeat dropped us two places to sixth, the lowest we had been since August. The following weekend there was a break from League Two action as we entertained Aldershot in the FA Cup. A top six position wasn't at all bad for a first season as a Football League member but there was still a distinct feeling that if we got beaten by Aldershot Micky might go. I felt it and so did the players. Surely there was no way it was going to happen. Aldershot were struggling at the wrong end of the division and in my time at Fleetwood we had never lost three games on the trot.

Well, we did lose three. Aldershot stunned us by playing well-above their League position. A brilliant thirty yard strike by Peter Vincenti on half time gave them a 2-1 lead after we had gone ahead through Junior Brown. It was a real body blow and they went through to the Third Round 3-2.

As I was driving home, I got a call from Micky to tell me that he'd been sacked. Despite the result and recent disappointments it still came as a massive shock after everything we'd achieved at the club. For me it was traumatic. I was not in a strong place mentally and emotionally after

Mum's death and my friendship with Micky stretched back years. It was as if I'd been hit by another hammer blow and I really felt for my old mate. An intense but exciting period had come to an end. There had been pressure to succeed but we had come through to achieve the dream of reaching the Football League. There had been many games played with real edge and passion. In the end we lost three consecutive times and it did for my old mate. What had been a strong relationship and friendship with the Chairman had eroded for various reasons. Many in the football world thought the decision had been made too early without understanding what had gone on behind the scenes. The relationship between Chairman and manager could not be healed and Andy Pilley ended it.

Over the next few days we were all going through the motions. Craig Madden and Steve Macauley took over temporarily and the waiting game led to lots of rumours and speculation. Every player and staff member could be affected by a new appointment. Those in the team might suddenly feel vulnerable while others on the fringe were given hope. It's human nature and there was the added thought that if a certain person got the job, you as a player could be on the way because of previous encounters. The appointment of a new manager affects everyone, not least backroom staff who are left wondering if a new guy will bring his own in.

Andy Pilley turned to a young management team of former Preston North End duo, Graham Alexander and Chris Lucketti. I had previously worked with Chris in my brief spell at Huddersfield Town and he and Graham were two of the most respected professionals in the game. 'Grezza' had made over 1000 appearances in his career. He was a penalty specialist who scored with his very last touch in football.

Despite my allegiance to Micky Mellon I had no axe to grind with Graham or Chris. After a nil-nil against Southend at home, we embarked on what was to be the second of my three journeys to forget. Gillingham away was a nightmare. We set off on the Friday morning at nine 'o'clock and returned at eleven on Saturday night. We got a good draw against a side who would go up as champions but I sat on my own on the coach, bored stiff and despondent. It was ten days before Christmas and I had no time for Christmas shopping or being with my family.

The third unfortunate away game was to Oxford United. It was on the eve of the Christmas festivities and we had a wasted journey. We arrived in the Oxford area on Friday and the game was called off during Saturday morning. Instead of a potential opportunity to get back home in good time, it was decided that the lads would stop off at Stoke on the way back and we trained in the pouring rain.

One of my lecturers used to work for a Super League club in rugby league. One day, I asked him why he had given up,

'I was coming home one day and listening to the banter in the team bus and realised that I didn't want it anymore.'

I didn't understand his thinking at the time but after my trips to Dagenham and Redbridge, Gillingham and Oxford I began to understand what he was saying. Graham wanted and needed to stamp his own authority on the club and, inevitably, this meant changes. That's his prerogative. It all ended for me in January 2013. The gaffer just pulled me to one side and told me that he had had a long think and decided to release me. Steve Macauley was going as well.

'I know you wouldn't want to be a number two', he told me. I was an easy option to go because I was self-employed. Compensation-wise you are entitled to a couple of weeks, that's all. I just walked out of the De Vere Hotel in Blackpool after the lads had a session in the gym and didn't look back. I wasn't the sort to hang around and shake hands. It wasn't my style. The players who really cared and who knew me well rang or texted. The rest couldn't give a toss because they were just out to look after themselves. People move on all the time in football. It's no big deal. As ever at times like this, things were left in the air. I was in the middle of organising Andy Mangan's rehab, for instance . . . . but that's life.

This was the fourth time I had been sacked and it's not nice when you've not done anything wrong, mistreated anyone or been unprofessional.

The first one, at Oldham, I contributed to myself. Stoke was one I manufactured myself. Huddersfield pissed me off. I would like to have seen the season out with Fleetwood Town but it wasn't to be. The double trauma of losing Mum and Micky's sacking convinced me that I was ready once again to leave football in a full-time capacity. I was prepared to turn my back on the intensity of winning games on a knife-edge, the last-minute goals and the unbelievable adrenaline rush. It's an addiction which is difficult to break from but now it was time for pastures new. As for Micky, he was soon back in the game alongside Dave Flitcroft at Barnsley and they masterminded a fantastic recovery to keep their side in the Championship in 2013. I was delighted for him.

I wasn't out of the game for long. After the excitement of helping Fleetwood into the Football League I moved to the more modest surroundings of Stainton Park where Radcliffe Borough play in the Evo Stik Division One North. It was proper grass roots football. Stainton Park lies between the M61 and M66 motorways north of Manchester so it wasn't far from home and a place I knew well.

Some of my private work was based at the clinic at Radcliffe. My old mate Ronnie Evans from the 'MASH' unit was also there. Ronnie had been physio at Stainton Park for about sixteen years and involved in the setting up of a Sports Injury Clinic about seven years ago. Ronnie is an absolute diamond and a loyal friend who fights in your corner and is one of the best mates that I have in football. He had been badgering me for some time to go and join him. In the end I gave in and went into a partnership for the first time in my career. There was real potential there with masses of local sports teams and a need for good quality treatment for injuries. Ronnie did most of the work and I would go in on Monday and Thursday afternoons, see some patients and help train the team in the evening.

I had also been going along for a while on a free Saturday and watching Radcliffe's games. Friends ran the club and I would share a drink with them afterwards. I was asked if I was interested in helping out on match day. On the football side, there was just Ronnie and manager Kevin Glendon who I've known for a long time. Kevin was a midfield player with Hyde United and Mossley. He had a long association with

Radcliffe stretching back over twenty years. As well as being manager, Kevin was also responsible for raising money to keep the club afloat. It's through Kevin's efforts that grants from the likes of the Football Association and the Lottery Fund have been secured to produce decent facilities on and off the field. Then there were the annual golf days. Bernard Manning's son is the chairman at Radcliffe and Bernard senior often used his contacts to get big names involved. Believe it or not, City-mad Bernard had a very good friendship with Sir Alex Ferguson and Fergie would sometimes appear. Bernard would order Fergie about when he came and ribbed him if he was late. Not many can say they've done that!

Stainton Park has a decent pitch, the social club has a function room and sports bar, there are floodlit Astroturf pitches and newish changing facilities. In fact there are quite a few changing rooms because of the extensive use of the Astroturf by local groups. These separate sections looked after themselves. It was just the football that wasn't paying its way. There was a limited budget so it wasn't possible to attract more decent players.

I was basically told to do what I wanted while Kevin coached and selected. He brought me into the strategic side and I had a greater input into tactics than I've had at the bigger clubs I've worked at. With Ronnie and my expertise we had a physio set-up far ahead of others in the league! Ronnie moved across to assistant manager as well. He told me that all he did was text players the times for training and matches and they turned up.

Ronnie and I gave words of encouragement and it usually worked out well. He was the quieter support for the lads and I was the voice, as I had been at previous clubs. I still found it easy to get animated on match day and with not many fans watching the games you could hear me right across the pitch! I knew that I had to be careful and take a step back but I still got agitated just like I did at Oldham Athletic. I will always set high standards. It might have been a part-time role to help a couple of mates at a modest level in the football pyramid but I still found that I had to give it my all. I would ask myself,

'Why can't I settle down and watch like most people do?'

Kevin would then turn round and say, 'Because that's not you.'

Players at the top are fit, talented and mentally strong. As you go down the leagues, you notice that one or two of those components will be missing. That's what separates the Premier League and international stars from the rest. One of the major factors in non-league football, for instance, is a relative lack of fitness compared to the top level. When you are not fit you tire, overstretch for the ball, lose co-ordination and end up injured. If you lose strength you can't fight a challenge off.

The players at this level cannot learn as fast as the stars. They keep making the same mistakes week-in, week-out and are not able to train full-time to put them right. I quickly found that individual errors cost Radcliffe games where we had been better than the opposition for long periods. You had to be tolerant of working with players of more modest ability and I'm not sure I fully learnt to be this way. Ronnie is different. His attitude is more along the lines of 'He's doing the best he can, that's all we've got. We've got to coax him.' Fitness is another key part.

I was still in football which was the main thing and really enjoyed being involved at such a decent club amongst people I knew well. The travelling was not as great as I'd been used to. It was largely north-west based like in the early days with Fleetwood Town but we did go as far as Darlington. Radcliffe Borough will never win the league as long as they're up against big teams like Darlo. Nevertheless, the set-up at the club made it easier for me to establish routines. It was basically just match days and training on certain nights. That is one of the joys of non-league. You can plan your life accordingly round set days.

Chapter Twenty-One

TREATING INJURIES

'You saved my life that day'

Dealing with injuries is the nitty-gritty of a physiotherapist's life. You look at the game in a different way from anyone else at the ground. A corner comes in, everyone challenges in the area and the ball is headed away. All eyes are on play as it moves upfield but the physio will always be looking back to see if there are any bodies left on the ground. I have been fortunate in that there haven't been too many really bad injuries to deal with in my career. However, if you are squeamish I suggest you move on to the next chapter!

One memorable incident from early in my career featured the former Northern Ireland international David McCreery at Newcastle United. It was in the early stages of a game against Bolton Wanderers at St. James' Park. David collapsed after coming together with Peter Haddock in a challenge on Bolton's Neil Whatmore near the half way line. Haddock was clearly hurt as well but my attention was on David who was screaming. Arthur Cox and I rushed to his aid. When I got to him there was no blood but you could see inside his leg and his knee joint was visible. David had been raked by a stud which had literally sliced his thigh open. It didn't seem to be an intentionally aggressive incident but David, with his distinctive long hair, was flat out on the pitch in agony.

Arthur Cox was standing near David's head as I got to work. Suddenly, David started groaning even more and Arthur asked him if he was ok.

'No I'm not! You're stood on my fucking hair!'

'Well, you should get it bloody cut then!'

They were taking people out of the crowd who had fainted with the shock. You could see the glistening white muscle sheath but everyone thought it was his bone sticking out. David was obviously in pain and discomfort. I tried to cover the area and arranged for a stretcher to be brought on. Eventually one appeared but it took a while. It should have been in the tunnel near where David had gone down but Arthur had removed it. We tracked it down to the little treatment room near the changing room. Arthur had had a bad injury which finished his own career and was superstitious. He didn't like the sight of a stretcher which is why it wasn't where it should have been. It wouldn't be allowed to happen in the modern game but back then Cox ruled the club with an iron fist. He was very much the old-fashioned type of manager. What he said went.

The club surgeon came to all home games and was there in the changing room when I arrived with David. We arranged for an ambulance and an operation that night. David had over fifty stitches but was back playing within a month. It was the type of injury that wasn't as bad as it looked. As soon as the wound had healed and mobility returned he was on the pitch again.

My old mate Billy Urmson ran on with the bag for reserve games at Oldham. Billy was hilarious. I used to watch the game from within a sponsor's box while he was on duty. It gave me easy access to the pitch via the tunnel if I was needed and was a welcome shelter from the freezing cold conditions which so often happened at Boundary Park. I'd be in there with Joe and usually one or two directors.

One day Billy ran on to the pitch to attend to Alex Jones, a young centre half who had suffered a bang on the head. Billy got to Alex and suddenly started screaming! I realised that there was something badly wrong and dashed out of the box, on to the pitch and across to the injured lad. Alex appeared to have a big gash above the eyebrow which made it flap over the eye and hang down. It looked as if his eye had come out and it had panicked Billy. I applied some dry compression bandages, cupped the hanging bit in my hand and put it back in place. Then I told Alex to hold it. He thinks he's going to die by this stage. I reassured him that there was no great damage. 'It's a straightforward five-minute job.' Then I left it to the doctor. I told Billy that under no circumstances must he scream when attending a player! It would have been much better to turn and wave me on.

You have to calm situations down at times like that. The first aid training emphasises it. When you are running on to that field of play you don't know what you are going to be confronted with. You cannot and shouldn't jump to any conclusions even though you've seen countless types of injury through your career. You usually have an idea about what part is injured from a distance but even so I've been on to a pitch before and asked a player:

'Is it your knee?'

'No, it's my ankle.'

A lad called Brian Adams fractured his thigh when playing for Oldham's youth team. Again Billy went on. I followed because I knew Billy needed help. There was no screaming from my colleague this time, though. He had learnt his lesson! Brian's thigh was mis-shapen and the lad was in a great deal of pain. It was definitely a hospital job. They operated quickly but Brian never really came back. He played local non-league after that and was working for an insurance company last time I saw him.

Another very visual injury was the one received by Fleetwood Town's former midfielder, Jamie McGuire, in a Conference game at Cambridge United two or three years ago. Jamie went down in their penalty area and when I got to him I noticed a big dint on the side of his face. It was quite obvious that he had damaged his cheekbone. In my early days I would have walked him off like a gladiator but, instead, Jamie had to be fitted with a neck brace and carried off. To be honest, this can actually be uncomfortable if there is a fracture of the cheekbone but there we go. It's more than my job's worth to ignore the guidance. Jamie had an operation but, fortunately, didn't need a face mask. He got the predictable banter from his mates, particularly the Scousers who were hoping he would have a mask because he was frightening enough to look at as it was!

Escorting Fleetwood Town's Rob Atkinson off the pitch
(Picture courtesy of Mark Wilson, FTFC)

You sometimes have to think on your feet. A perfect example was that of Jeff Clarke who was a centre half at Newcastle. Jeff took a bad knock with about twenty minutes to go and when I reached him his nose was on the other side of his face. Arthur Cox was screaming from the side, 'He's not coming off!'

Jeff said to me, 'Is my nose broken?' I said that it wasn't, treated him and ran off. He must have headed twenty or thirty balls in the last part of the game. He came off the pitch, got into the changing room, looked in the mirror and nearly fainted.

'You told me it wasn't broken,' he said.

'You wouldn't have headed those balls if I'd told you it was.'

'You bastard.'

I turned away trying not to laugh! Jeff must have learnt something that day because after retiring he studied for a physiotherapy degree at Salford University and started a new career.

Another centre-half, Oldham's Andy Linighan, had a recurring issue. If the ball hit a certain spot on his head it could trigger a reaction and he would start to wander off towards right or left back. I would immediately turn to Joe and say:

'He's at it again, boss'.

I got him smelling salts and cold compresses at half time to bring him round. Then I sent him back out. That wouldn't happen today. One of the great myths of the game is the effect of the 'magic sponge' when treating players. The cold water would always get an instant reaction. That's all it was. You wouldn't do it now because of health and safety. Back then you put the soaking sponge to the cut until it stopped bleeding. Well it wouldn't ever stop because you need a dry compress to do that. Blood could be all over the place and then, when you finished, the sponge went back into the dirty water ready to be used again. These days cuts can be glued pitchside.

Football is a physical game and the risk of a player swallowing his tongue in a collision is always there. Ronnie Evans and I have both experienced such an occasion. I was with Oldham at the time. Hull City's Andy Payton had collided with our goalkeeper. On arrival, I saw that our player had not much wrong with him but Andy was clearly displaying signs of struggling to breathe. Their physio tried to get him into the recovery position and I went over and tilted Andy's head which automatically released the tongue. Andy immediately settled down so I went back to my keeper before leaving the field with their physio. When

I went to Burnley some years later I met up with Andy again. He said straight away:

'You saved my life that day when you tilted my head. I'll never forget that.'

It was a thought that had honestly not crossed my mind at the time. I was just doing my job, reacting to a potentially dangerous situation in a calm and controlled manner. Many have tried to pull the tongue out of the throat but you shouldn't have to. It's so slippy it's virtually impossible. I've even been told about people using a pair of scissors to prise the mouth open. Tilting the head always works unless the player has an obstruction or is fitting. When Ronnie went on to attend his at Radcliffe, the player was fitting. Luckily there was a doctor in the crowd and between them they saved the day.

When I was at Accrington Stanley they started this business of taking the player off to the touchline for treatment. Play carries on and you are down to ten men. I think as much as anything it was to stop players going down willy-nilly. A player might now have to wait for thirty seconds to come back on. It only takes a second to score a goal. I always try to get my players to understand,

'If you go down it might be sore. I know because I've been there myself. It's much better, though, to shake it off, get up and show me you are ok. Give me the thumbs up. I don't want to go on unless you are really injured.'

I had to train them into that way of thinking but it took time with some of them. The youngsters in particular needed to understand that you can't keep going over and over. There were a couple at Accrington who would be down three or four times a game. I would get to them and they would be getting up. I'd say 'What's up with you?' They'd reply, 'He kicked me'.

'Well go and kick him back. You've got to avoid coming off with me.'

I can remember one Accrington game where one of our players went down on the far side. The referee called me on but I refused.

'Tell him to get up,' I shouted across. Immediately, the crowd started getting on at me. The lad did get up and I said to him after the game, 'You've really got to stop doing that.'

One way of spotting a serious injury is if the player is not moving. Fortunately, that scenario doesn't happen often. Gradually, you get used to your players to the extent that you know when they have a genuine problem or whether they are crying 'Wolf'. One thing I absolutely hate is when players fall down in a deliberate attempt to get other players booked. Joe Royle used to have plenty to say about that. He even considered the physics of it all:

'Why do players roll around after hitting the ground? Surely, there's not enough energy left to make a second roll. It's harder to roll than to lie there! They are doing it for effect and that's cheating.'

Joe would save a particular volley of criticism for goalkeepers who have a habit of doing it. It drove him mad. Injuries can frequently be used as a time-wasting exercise towards the end of a game while sides under a lot of pressure will deliberately tell someone to go down. It's a way of breaking up momentum. If the other team get into a rhythm and there is wave after wave of attack, there would be a shout from the technical area, 'Go down'. I used to be sent on to the pitch with all sorts of messages. 'Do this, do that . . . .' It was a way of a manager getting points to his players. I'd be giving so many messages that I would forget the player I'm supposed to have gone on for!

Treatment for Darren Beckford, Oldham Athletic

Treating injuries on the pitch can be a difficult enough business on its own without the added problems that can come with it. For a start there are referees who will often try to rush you. You have a perfect excuse on your side though.

'This player is injured and I need to do a proper assessment before I can move him.'

Referees don't have an answer to that because they know they could be in major trouble if they rush things and serious complications follow. Then there are the fans watching on. Dealing with them could be a harrowing business. Remember that a lot of the old grounds had standing on all sides which could be really close to the pitch and fans would push to the front if there was something kicking off between players.

I have lost count of the number of times I have been spat on and spat at whilst running round the touchline to or from an injury. It was disgusting. There's nothing worse than feeling a large gob of spit running down your back or into your face as a cretin has launched a mouthful in your direction. Sometimes I'd deliberately run back in front of the goal to avoid a hazardous few yards close up alongside the opposition's hard core of fans. Often there wasn't much space behind the net and I found staying on the pitch much easier. Coins were regularly thrown. It could be a real hazard if you were hit and you couldn't see them flying at you. I learnt to pick them up and pocket them, smiling up to the fans as I did it. That can't happen now because I'd be done for inciting them and probably end up with a fine.

Elland Road was a particularly threatening place. I was there one year with Newcastle United when Kevin Keegan went down injured in front of the Kop close to the goal. There was about five minutes left in a Milk Cup match in which Kevin had helped set up what appeared to be the winner. The Leeds fans were incensed so Kevin had fallen in absolutely the worst place on the field. Our biggest star was lying in front of thousands of baying fans. I ran on to treat him and a hail of coins and sharp objects including metal nuts immediately came our way. Kevin was hit just above the eye by a nut. I was hit on the head by a bolt and collected a bump for my troubles. We could both have lost our eyesight. The police came and had to put their capes over us for protection. I had to lead Kevin off down the touchline. It wasn't an easy journey. If that sort of behaviour happened now, the ground would be closed.

It wasn't the only time that I felt fear at Leeds United. We had to get off the pitch fast on another occasion. The Oldham Athletic fans were, for some reason, in seats under a section of Leeds supporters who were ripping seats out and throwing them down. Oldham fans spilled on to pitch, followed by the home supporters. I was treating someone on the far side, looked up and said words to the effect, 'I think we need to leg it!'

Vital to the role of the physio is his relationship with the manager and there was plenty of cat and mouse taking place when it came to dealing with injuries. Once your manager knows you are competent they will start to listen to you but you often have to battle to get your voice heard at first. When you are dealing with so many situations in such a passionate and demanding sport there are bound to be difficulties.

Most managers want players back from injury as soon as possible. However, I don't want them back playing too early and then returning to me injured again. I would constantly question myself,

'Should I have got him back by then, was it too quick, should I have left it longer . . . ?'

Joe Royle took a quite different stance at Oldham. I'd go into Joe's office and say,

'Joe, he's going to be out for two to three weeks.'

He'd reply, 'Just tell me when he's ready to come back. That's your job.'

In Joe's mind one player's injury gave another a chance. Joe had complete trust in my judgement which helped a lot. With other managers I would adopt different tactics,

'In my opinion he's going to be out for three weeks, boss.'

'Well I need him in two.'

In that instance you knew you had a deadline so I would deliberately start to put a little bit of extra time on my assessments to give myself a cushion.

From time to time there are fitness tests to supervise. Don't get me going on those! This involves taking a player through a set of exercises to determine whether or not he can play. First point to make—I'm dead against having them on the day of the game. You're either fit or you are not. On occasions, I've put players through a rigorous fitness test for fifteen minutes. They start the game and come off within half an hour.

I don't mind doing them on a Friday but prefer just special cases on the day of the match. I will say to the player after the test,

'Are you fit to do ninety minutes at a pace that we can't match in a fitness test?'

If I see any doubt I will say, 'I don't think you are, are you?'

Legally it's their decision. I cannot demand a player plays because he could break down. You shouldn't put yourself in that position.

'Are you fit to play?'

Pause from player . . .

'Are you fit to play for 90 minutes?'

'Not sure.'

'Right, we'll leave it another week and I'll go and tell the gaffer.'

There are loads of factors involved in determining fitness for a game. A player might say,

'If I play badly it might affect my move and I can't take that risk.'

Steam would be coming out of my ears by then. I'd go into the boss and say,

'I think he's ok but he says he's unfit to play.'

Then it would be in the manager's court. I've had players refuse to play because they are on loan and it isn't in their interest to play with a niggling injury. We've really needed that player. We're paying his wages but we can't push it. With every individual injury I have to manage the situation, set out a treatment and rehabilitiation plan and maintain levels of fitness during their time away from the game.

The treatment room can easily become a de-stabilising influence in a football club because of the mental state of the lads who might be in it, particularly the long-term injured. I saw one of my most important roles as being able to use my life experience to be honest and straight with the lads and keep their spirits up. A long period out of the game makes them more fragile and they need to be handled with great care.

As a physio you are between the players and the management. Players will share confidences with you that nobody else will hear, not even their loved ones. You can quickly earn their trust and it is a privileged position to be in. There is so much banter and joking when the lads are together but when the others are all out training or playing and you are left with the injured the reality of their situation kicks in. Confidence is low and doubts appear about when or whether they will play again.

What I call 'proper players' will ask, 'How long will this injury take to mend?' They want to know what they've done and what they have to do to put it right. The 'proper players' tend to be those you cannot do without. I can now give them my advice based on years of experience and using technology that has improved massively. There was no such thing as MRI scans when I first started, for instance. Grade One injuries are those which will need two to three weeks to sort out, grade two three to six weeks and grade three more than six weeks. Complete tears of ligaments, tendons, muscles and bones will come into this last category.

Some players can see their time on the physio's treatment table as a bit of a rest, particularly the more experienced pros. Stan Ternent had a lot of older, stronger characters at Burnley. Paul Cook was a case in point,

'I've got a bit of a tight hamstring, SOSS. Just need to stay with you for a few days. I'm not training until Thursday and by the way I'm not coming for treatment either. Sort it out with the boss will you. I'll be ok for Saturday. Cheers mate.'

I would go and tell Stan. Nine times out of ten he would say,

'Tell Cooky to have a few days off, then. Give him a rest, that's all right.'

Cooky never let you down on a Saturday. Getting players ready to win on match day is what it's all about. You can have players who do very little during the week but give you everything on a Saturday. You get to know the types of players. As they get older they need more individual programmes. There was no point in flogging Jon Parkin round long runs at Fleetwood Town. Instead, you tailored a programme that would get him out on Saturday. Other players generally accept it but one or two will say sarcastically,

'I can't wait to make thirty and get my days off.'

When they do get to that age some of them need to train every day otherwise they can't function. Others need more rest. Everyone is different. Each will have a different reaction to injury, both physically and mentally, a different recovery period. One of my favourite sayings to injured players is:

'What's your problem?'

'I can't run.'

'Bollocks,' I would reply, 'If a lion came through that door what would you do?'

'Run.'

'You can run then.'

Footballers at all levels hate running. If the weather is really bad and they cannot get on to the pitches, they know what lies in store. As I used to tell them, they have to run to play football. They don't mind running with a ball or chasing one but you give them any sort of distance to run and they will immediately complain. There were exceptions, of course. Terry McDermott would run for ever and was a top-class athlete. At the opposite extreme was Graham Branch at Burnley who hated running to the extent that he wouldn't sleep the night before if he knew it was running the following day. He eventually asked the doctor for sleeping pills.

I have even come across players who don't want to play! Sounds funny when it is their livelihood but perhaps the crowd has been on their backs, confidence might be low, family worries could be surfacing. In these situations, the manager might say,

'Let's take him out for a couple of weeks to keep him out of the spotlight'.

They'd come to me for a bit of a laugh and a joke and sit and watch some games. Watching football can often help you analyse where you are in your own game.

Sadly, and inevitably, some have been forced to retire through their injuries. The first time that I experienced this was at Newcastle and, touchingly, the lad concerned, Derek Bell, sent me a letter thanking me for my efforts. I've still got it:

> *Ian*
>
> *Just thought I'd write a few words to thank you for helping me in the last few years. It's just unfortunate that things haven't worked out as planned. Thanks for all the hard work you put me through and all the treatment you gave to me as you picked me up when I was down and got me back playing again. It's much appreciated and if there is any way in which I can repay you for what you did for me then you know where to come.*
>
> *These kind of things happen for a reason and I'm looking forward to my new career as it will give me good experience and stand me in good stead for the future and it still keeps me involved with sport.*
>
> *I'd like to wish you all the best for the future whatever you do and thanks for all you have done for me. Keep in touch.*
>
> *Yours gratefully*
>
> *PS you might win a game of head tennis now!*

It was a gesture that I won't forget. Derek was a midfield player who had a cruciate ligament problem in his knee but in those days they weren't diagnosed. He had operations but the joint was basically knackered. They just sewed him up then he tried rehab with me. He had to give up the game he loved in his teenage years.

That same injury can now be treated. Advances in technological and medical developments, many coming from America, have given players another chance. With the first anterior cruciate injuries in the knee that I had to deal with they put a synthetic ligament in. One player I came across, Oldham Athletic's Gary Hoolickin, found his body rejecting it and had it removed. Once that happened, the surgeons stopped using that procedure, now they use the back third of the patella or hamstring tendon and sew it to the bone. I still see Gary. There is no ligament in his knee and it will eventually need replacing. He fits kitchens now!

Another injury which never used to be diagnosed was a hernia and it would often finish a career. In 1980 Jerry Gilmore, a Harley Street surgeon, recognised a fairly common syndrome among sportsmen in kicking sports. The condition is also known as a Sports Hernia but a more apt title is the 'Gilmore Groin' because, strictly speaking, there is no herniation. He went where surgeons previously didn't go and now there are medics round the country operating on hernias. Suddenly sporting hernias are operable and careers can resume. This is all good news because the worst situation that you can come across is when a player's injuries get the better of him and the career that has meant everything to him is ended. Mercifully, it doesn't happen too often.

Chapter Twenty-Two

DISCIPLINARY PROBLEMS

Anyway what are you going to charge him with—assaulting a bucket?!

I am in a caring profession where a calm approach to injuries is a necessity. I have always done this well. However, my volatile side has come to the surface all too often and landed me in big trouble. When I first came into the game friendly banter with small crowds was the norm. At the bigger clubs, particularly Newcastle United, the atmosphere around the grounds was more intense. I coped most but not all of the time.

At Goodison Park, for instance, the Everton fans were really close to us in the technical area. One day I was there with Oldham Athletic and had coffee deliberately thrown in my face. Luckily it was warm not piping hot. I wiped it out of my eyes before having a go at the fella who threw it. The stewards came across immediately and tried to remove me. Suddenly we had the police involved. Joe Royle backed me up,

'What you charging him with? Having coffee thrown in his face? How do you expect him to react?'

Joe's favourite line when addressing an unruly fan was:

'Have they let you out for the day? What time are you due back?'

You could get away with it in those days. Anyway, I got a letter from the police saying that they weren't pursuing charges on the coffee issue but I still had to go in front of the FA who told me that I must never react, despite what happens.

The bench at Burnden Park was literally just a bench with no cover over it. We were playing Bolton Wanderers just after the article about me had appeared in the News of the World. A voice from the crowd shouted,

'Oy, Liversedge, whose wife are you shagging now?'

Instinctively, I pointed at the guy and shouted back, 'Yours!'

The whole of the bench collapsed in hysterics. Joe was beside himself with laughter. The fella's veins in his neck grew clearer but he couldn't come back with anything. That was the sort of fun we used to have. These days I would be done for inciting the crowd.

Arthur Cox had a habit of sending me round the pitch with a tie-up in my hand. It was really an excuse to get a message to a player.

'Go and tell whoever to do whatever,' was the gist and it nearly got me arrested at Rotherham. I had been sent round several times already during the game.

'Go and tell Waddle to shift his arse,' came the next command from Arthur. I headed off again with yet another tie-up. As I got behind the goal, Chris Waddle would trick me by walking back across to other side. He knew what was coming. I went backwards and forwards repeatedly! At the Newcastle end there was a cheer and a surge, at the Rotherham end I was verbally abused. I would mouth my messages to Chris and hope he got them. Then I'd get back into the dug-out and Arthur would say:

'Have you told him?'

'Yes, boss.'

On about the fourth attempt the referee finally interpreted my efforts to pass on the tie-up as touchline coaching. The story was covered in the local press:

> *'Newcastle United felt the brunt of the police's get-tough policy on October 2 when club physiotherapist Ian Liversedge seemed to almost come under arrest due to a misunderstanding at Rotherham's Millmoor ground.*
>
> *Macclesfield referee John Hough interpreted Liversedge's attempt to pass on a tie-up on the far side of the pitch as touchline coaching.*
>
> *The official immediately ordered him back to his seat in the dug-out.*
>
> *Two police officers went one step further and escorted him through a perimeter fence into a compound housing a police detention hut.'*

The players thought it was hilarious. Arthur took me to the changing room after the game to clarify my story. A Newcastle director pulled me during the following week and asked me to explain why I was doing the trips backwards and forwards from the dug-out. I told him.

'You won't be doing that again,' he told me, much to my relief.

South Yorkshire police were adamant that spectators were not to be provoked, there was to be no dissent and the game should be played in the proper spirit. They were worried about foul language, the use of 'V' signs and arguing with the referee at the county's five league grounds. Sometime after the incident, the Assistant Chief Constable told a press conference that, so far, no players had been arrested in South Yorkshire but a visiting team official had been reported to his club and reprimanded.

The club was Newcastle United, the venue was Rotherham and the official was me!

Arthur threw a punch at me at Cardiff once because I'd argued with the referee. They had a massive centre half, I think it was Phil Dwyer, who dumped Peter Beardsley on to the cinder track that went round Ninian Park. Anyway, I got to Peter and all his leg's grazed. I had a right go with Roger Milford the referee. I think he took my name because I had pushed it too far. I always had to have the last word. Back in the dug-out, Arthur asked if Milford had booked me. I said he had and Arthur aimed the punch. Willie McFaul had us both at arm's length. It was near the end of the game and the row continued afterwards. Arthur physically dragged me in off the pitch. We went straight to Roger Milford's room.

'Have you booked him?' asked Arthur. 'If so we'll deal with it at club level.'

I was suggesting to Roger, 'Tell him you've booked me,' because I preferred to get the sack than be treated like this. Milford said that he hadn't but I knew he had. We went back into our changing room. Kevin Keegan threw a boot at us.

'We've just had wins at Swansea and Cardiff in four days and this is how you two behave.' I was prepared to go back to the north-east by train but one or two players persuaded me to go on coach. It was a long and silent journey.

I was in the next day treating injuries. Arthur Cox pulled me into his room. I was going to tell him to stick his job but Arthur was great at taking the wind out of people's sails. He said,

'What are we like, SOSS? What was all that about yesterday?'

I deflated in front of him. Keeping calm, I had my say about the referee and we got on with things. That happened a lot with Arthur.

Although I practised it often, I never regretted stepping in. There was no attempt to be malicious. It was all part of the adrenalin that football aroused inside me. I also felt that I was protecting my players by reacting. If one of the opposition kicked one of my players I'd go on the pitch and have a go at them. I had a go at referees for letting it happen. Kicking my player is like kicking me. I was so involved. I kicked and headed every ball, especially when I was younger.

I've had to learn lessons and my abrasive style eventually got me the push from Oldham. I remember a Latics game, against Stan Ternent's Hull City at Boothferry Park. Hull got a penalty when Andy Payton was brought down. There was a bucket of water near the dug-out and I got up and instinctively booted it on to the pitch. Joe told me to go and get it back. I picked it up. The fans were caged in behind us, where the idiots always seemed to be, faces pressed up against the fence, snarling.

Something inside me told me to aim to throw water at them even thought the bucket was empty. I swung the bucket at them and they all ducked. I turned the bucket upside down and grinned at them!

They scored the penalty and I booted the bucket back on. Next thing this police inspector has come up. The game was still on but he wanted to take me away for inciting the crowd. Joe defended me:

'Leave him alone, he's our physio. Anyway what are you going to charge him with—assaulting a bucket?!'

Some mates later told me that the incident was featured on the national radio commentary of the game:

'Hull awarded a penalty, there's a bucket on the pitch. GOAL! The bucket's back on the pitch.'

I had loads of people come up later asking if it was me! Anyway, half time came and they still wanted to arrest me. Joe Royle and Stan Ternent were involved in an argument with the police about inciting the crowd. Joe got me out of it, yet again, and the incident showed that things were never straightforward where Andy Payton was concerned!

There were certain clubs where you just knew you were in for trouble. Both Millwall and Stoke City fans were noted for problems. Millwall's Old Den was intimidating from the word go. We always had to have an armoured police escort in front and behind the coach as the approach to the ground was through an estate. Police advice was simple, just keep driving! Everyone was told to either sit in the centre seats or in the aisle. The crowd weren't just young kids but grown men and some had the youngsters with them, clones of their dads. In the end we used to laugh at them because we had protection from stewards and the police. The New Den improved because it was an all-seater and in a different area.

Attacks on the coach were rare but when they happen I certainly remember them clearly! AEK Athens fans stoned the Newcastle coach after a pre-season 'friendly' in Greece. Once Kevin Keegan went to St. James' Park, Newcastle became an attractive team for games like that everywhere but that was a rather scary departure from the ground. We made up for it with a great evening out, though! We went into a night club and suddenly a plane flew right over the top. Until that point I hadn't noticed there was no roof on the building! We watched some plate dancing. It was a traditional Greek tradition and involved the audience. Needless to say, it didn't take long to get me up on stage!

I was involved in many altercations in technical areas. Joe called it 'the battle of the bench' at Boundary Park! The players would go out and he would say to me,

'You ready for the battle of the bench, mate?'

Problems would often spread into the tunnel at half-time and full-time. I chased Bradford's Terry Dolan down the tunnel once at Oldham after an argument on the touchline. He locked the dressing room door and I tried to get in but Joe saved me from anything worse! I still see Terry today and we have a laugh about it.

One of my less-pleasurable episodes at Boundary Park was when one of the local officers told lies about me. I was charged with abusing a fourth official and the policeman wrote a purely fabricated statement. I was pulled up in front of the FA and I was livid. I didn't expect policemen to lie. He had been close by and witnessed the argument. The FA said that they weren't interested in what I'd said but more the fact that the policeman had picked this up. He said that I'd racially abused the official and I knew that I hadn't. The long-running feud led me to appear before the Chief Superintendent in Chadderton. Oldham Chairman, Ian Stott, tried to calm things down. In a written statement I stuck to my guns and intimated that I was prepared to take it further. The policeman and I had to sit down together and try to thrash it out.

I was always in trouble. I just had to push my luck and test people's patience. I had been a fiery player with a short fuse and carried it on into my career as a physio. I even went to anger management classes at one stage and it worked. The key word was 'WASP'—wait, assess, slowly proceed. I think Dad used to despair of me and would regularly say:

'When are you going to learn?'

Jean, my second wife, came out with the classic line,

'Ever since I've known you you've been paying a fine!'

One of my last transgressions came at Accrington Stanley when I called the fourth official a 'prick' and copped yet another FA fine. The club paid it I think. The Accrington touchline was always a lively place to be. The management team of John Coleman and Jimmy Bell were constantly winding the officials up and getting sent to the stands. I remember one occasion when John almost finished up in a touchline fight with Terry Brown of Aldershot. On another, Macclesfield Town were playing us at the Crown Ground and their manager, Paul Ince, hit one of our players, Leam Richardson, in front of the fourth official. Leam had picked the ball up to take a throw in. Ray Mathias, Macclesfield's assistant manager, was shouting instructions when Leam ran up and barged into him. Ray was knocked over and I had no doubt that Leam did it on purpose. Everyone got involved and Ince threw a punch over the top which caught Leam on the back of his head. I was incensed.

There had been previous between the sides. Only the season before Andy Mangan had scored a late equaliser at Macclesfield. Mangs had been celebrating up the line when Ince tripped him as he went past.

Back at Accrington, the incident with Leam ended up with both John and Jimmy getting sent to the stand. I was left alone in the technical area but because the Crown Ground was so tight they were actually in the front row next to me! I started to have a go at the fourth official. He said to me,

'If you say anything else I'll call the referee over.'

At the end of the game, the fourth official was standing outside the changing room in the corner of the ground. I called him a 'prick' and he reported me. I got a letter, which I put with the others, and a fine.

It was from around that time that I approached things in a different way. I was still passionate at the likes of Huddersfield Town, Hyde and Fleetwood Town. I still wanted to protect my players but lessons had been learned. Gradually, I came to the conclusion that referees are human and make mistakes. Some are worse than others and the really bad ones usually end up the same for both sides. The lower you go down the pyramid, the less good the referees are. Unless there's a horrendous decision which affects a game I'll leave things alone now. Arguing the toss takes you away from your job in hand. If a team loses it's not the referee's fault. Trouble is, I've always been a bad loser!

Chapter Twenty-Three

A LONG TEN MONTHS

It's the only time that I've been successful in a play-off and it was an immense feeling.

Football seasons seem to get longer and longer. Daily training, travelling, staying over for games, going through the range of emotions together all take their toll. It can be a 24/7 existence for ten months of the year. In addition, the play-offs have kept the season going for many clubs with an extra fortnight tagged on. A lot of physios outside the game have asked me,

'Why do you bother?'

It's a good question but the answer is that it is in my blood.

Pre-season seems to be on you in no time. It's the first stage of the new campaign and as the players gather the fans are high with expectation again. They will have scanned the fixture lists, made their arrangements, bought their season tickets and paraded their new strip.

Pre-season has become a lot more scientific. Previously, players would finish at the end of April and holiday until mid-July after which you never saw a ball for a fortnight. You would just run and run. Clubs are now in the habit of arranging individual fitness and dietary programmes over the summer before the players gather for a battery of tests which produce a stack of data about their pre-season fitness. This is always a tough period which players hate apart from just a few masochists who seem to like punishing themselves with bleep tests, fat index measures and the like. There is time away at camp and initiation tests to look forward to for new signings. Hope is in the air and players know that it's a new start and whatever went on last season is behind them. There may be a new gaffer to impress, the tan is topped up and they can't wait to start doing what they do best.

Friendly fixtures might give an indication or two on how the manager is thinking but everyone will get a crack and gain valuable match time. As the opening day arrives, players are more than ready and raring to go. Stage two begins and the season starts. The sun continues to shine and the pitches are looking like you'd want your lawn to look at home. Teams slowly settle to their new challenge. Managers with early success will guard against being over-optimistic.

'There's a long way to go. It's a marathon not a sprint.'

Managers of struggling teams will tell supporters not to read too much into it.

'There's a long way to go. These are early days.'

Teams will hopefully be injury-free, expectations will remain high, there will be a small gap between top and bottom in the league table.

The arrival of October brings the next stage and the sacking season begins. Reality begins to set in and the early hopes are beginning to fade. Managers might not have reached the goals set during the summer, perhaps the players brought in aren't delivering for one reason or another. If players are not in the side they get unsettled and start moaning, 'The manager's shit'.

Micky Mellon used to say, 'If you were playing well you'd be in the team. You are out of it because you're not playing well.' Joe Royle worked on the same principle. Unsettled players want to move on and their mood can affect others.

The clocks go back, the nights draw in. That starts to affect your afternoon plans. The weather changes, temperatures plummet, you are suddenly playing in rain or heavy wind. Pitches become lusher and slower while the training pitches can get unplayable, especially at the lower league levels. You hunt around for alternatives, a 3G artificial surface here, perhaps a 4G there. Too much training on such surfaces can affect joints and some players have to be kept off as a precaution. If you want to lay your own it costs a fortune. In days gone by we trained on anything. My old mate Craig Madden said that he used to train on a car park under street lights and I certainly remember training on hard surfaces like that. When we had the artificial pitch at Oldham we had a ready-made training surface for bad weather but that was an exception. Before that was put down, players came in and sat around while we rang here and there looking for an alternative.

As their hopes start to fade, fans moan. Only one team can win the league, don't they know. God, they are fickle. Results affect numbers through the gate which, in turn, affects revenue. Chairmen's minds begin to get made up. Occasionally, you can get a realistic chairman who knows exactly where the club is at and what building blocks need to be put in place long term but this seems to be more of a rarity these days. Too many succumb to pressure and pull the trigger. Joe was an exception at Oldham. He was given twelve years by an understanding Chairman and built the club up. These days, managerial sackings come thick and fast and dominate conversations all too often in the months up to Christmas. It's a merry-go round and clubs finish up paying costly compensation packages. There is no loyalty any more. Unless the manager is totally useless there should be some stability. If you didn't have an interest in the game and were looking from a distance you'd think it was shambolic and comical.

Once in, the new broom begins to sweep clean and every player in the squad considers how it will affect him. Those in the team wonder if they'll keep their place, others on the edge get renewed hope. A new manager draws in his own staff around him.

Thoughts begin to turn towards the January transfer window but before then we reach the next stage, the Christmas period. I love Christmas. Christmas puts a smile on faces. My birthday is on Boxing Day and I always celebrate with a game then go out afterwards. Players often have to train on Christmas Day. I never minded going in, to be fair. It would be an hour, maybe an hour and a half tops in the morning so it was no great sacrifice. In my thirty-one years in the game I can count the number of free Christmas Days on the fingers of one hand.

We tried all sorts of combinations around the fixtures, including taking teams away on December 25th. Players would have Christmas morning with family before going off to their hotel. I've stayed in many a hotel over Christmas and New Year.

One year Oldham had an eleven 'o' clock kick off on New Year's Day so Joe took us off to a hotel the night before. It was just down the road from the ground and there were three separate parties on! The lads went up around midnight and the rooms vibrated with the effects of three separate PA systems. I never wanted to hear 'Nellie the Elephant' again after that experience! I decided to spend the night elsewhere. I went through the ritual of wishing everyone Happy New Year before sneaking off down the fire escape and was back for breakfast. Looking around the group it was as if the lads had been up all night. We were two down in the first fifteen minutes.

Willie Donachie used to reckon the players were better off in their own beds but Joe took the view that they were young and impressionable lads who couldn't be trusted to stay at home and get an early night. Talking of trust, at Burnley Stan used to go mad when players ate too much on away trips. There would be soup and sandwiches on the way down on the coach followed by a meal at the hotel. Some would be ordering room service such as Burger and chips at eleven o'clock before breakfast next morning and a pre-match meal. They were like little boys in a sweet shop. Stan went ballistic.

'Would you eat like that at home?'

'No boss.'

'Well, why now?'

Those who ate the most were no use to anyone on match day. The management used to have to be on food patrol and strict guidelines.

Christmas can be hard. In my last season at Fleetwood Town I had just one day off. However, once it is over it is time to face up to potentially the two hardest months. By the time January starts you have all been together, living out of each other's pockets, for six months. It becomes a hard slog. The weather is still bad, often with snow and ice adding to the problems. You are going to and from work in the dark, the effects of a lot of travelling and constant effort are really kicking in and resistance is lowered. Injuries and illnesses result and players can fall away after starting the season well. To counter that, managers start a mini pre-season to boost fitness levels and keep players on their toes.

It is around this time that the countdown starts. Players start ticking the days off before the end of the season and their week in the sun. Over this four month period they can tell you in days how long there is before they go to Magaluf or Tenerife. Others perhaps count in weeks. I'm sure some had a chart up on the wall at home. It's a way of keeping them going, particularly if they're not getting a lot of football. It relieves the monotony. Despite training hard, players still have plenty of time to themselves and can easily succumb to temptation.

Gambling has been a classic example for footballers over the years and there have been some high profile cases of the effects of betting. Nowadays, with online betting, players can fritter away thousands in a single coach journey and there are some who have got themselves into serious difficulties because of their activities.

Back to the season and March and April put a spring in the step. It's getting lighter and milder now and the hour goes forward. Weather-ravaged pitches are on the mend and you might finally get back on to the training ground for the business end of the season.

There will be three basic situations facing you by this stage. You are hoping to go up, avoiding relegation or be somewhere in between. In my long career I've sampled all three.

To experience promotion is just the sweetest feeling and when Newcastle went up to the old First Division in 1984 it sparked massive celebrations on Tyneside. When we travelled down the A1 for away games we would watch in amazement as the Toon Army hung out of car windows and the back of vans with their bottles of Brown Ale and wave at the team coach! They certainly knew how to party.

Many say that the best way up is to win the play-off final. One of the biggest joys I have experienced in football was when Fleetwood Town won in the Conference North play-off final against Alfreton Town. It's the only time that I've been successful in a play-off and it was an immense feeling. The emotion experienced that day almost made getting into the Football League an anti-climax with us not actually playing when it finally happened.

The play-off system came into being in the mid-eighties. There is no doubt that it has enabled more teams to keep their season alive as four in each league have the chance to go into a knockout system with the winner taking the final promotion place. If you'd asked me of its value back at the start I would have looked at it a lot differently.

In the 1986-97 season, the very first time the new system came in, Oldham finished three points behind Portsmouth in the old Second Division, seven ahead of Leeds United in fourth. Previously we would have gone up automatically. As it was, we had to face Leeds in a two-legged semi-final with Ipswich and Charlton contesting the other. We had comfortably beaten all those teams in the league table but play-offs were soon to show us that league positions don't always matter.

We blew our chances against our old rivals from across the Pennines by relaxing. Leeds had won 1-0 at Elland Road with a late goal from Keith Edwards. Back at Oldham, Gary Williams brought us level as early as the 18th minute. It was game on and when Mike Cecere gave us the lead in the 89th minute we all headed off to celebrate with our fans. We committed the cardinal error of taking our minds off the game. Leeds went straight down to the other end and scored themselves, through Edwards again. It was a surreal moment. You could see it happening and it was like it was in slow motion. Some of our players were still celebrating, facing the stands with their arms in the air. Leeds put the ball down, kicked off, bang, back of net. It was an unbelievably cruel experience.

At Burnley we missed the play-offs three seasons in a row and I'm sure we went into the last game on one or two of those. By then things are chopping and changing by the minute and the fans are all glued to their radios.

Experiencing relegation is simply the worst experience ever. It happened twice to me, at Stoke and Oldham. This is the other side of the coin. You just feel flat, want the season to end and get away from the club. At Stoke, as I've already said, the last season affected me so much that I couldn't stomach the thought of going back. At Oldham we lost our coveted Premier League place but it was so much different. I felt part of the family and took it on the chin. After all, we had experienced the joy of going up. If we didn't get back it had been a great experience to have been there, going to all the great, romantic grounds every other week.

Mid-table obscurity used to allow you to blood youngsters and look to the future. It still happens but with all the scandal surrounding betting scams these days it has become less-advisable to field full teams of young players.

And so, another season ends. A small minority of clubs have achieved, others have plummeted while the majority live to fight another day. All these thoughts are a long way from the minds of players as their personal countdown ends and they are off on holiday.

Chapter Twenty-Four

HOLIDAY TIME

*'All I can remember is Frank picking people off my
back and slinging them across the pavement'*

 T ime to let your hair down and who better to do it with than the very
same people you have lived with for ten months! It was nice and simple
for the players. Bring your passport and beer money to the airport and
we're off. Destination? Magaluf, Tenerife, Corfu . . . .

You report to the airport, check in, have a few drinks at the bar followed
by a few more on the flight. At the other end you get off the plane,
dump your stuff, then it's out for more drinking. You arrange to meet
the following day at, say, eleven 'o' clock. The day after that it would
be twelve, and the time would gradually get later over the rest of the
holiday as people dropped off the pace.

I remember Tenerife once. Andy Goram turned up. He was at Rangers
by then and I think he had been sent out after injury for recuperation.
We were at a roadside bar and he walked by with his partner, baby and
mother-in-law. We shouted him over and he handed the kid over before
walking across to us. He told us he was out for a stroll but would be
flying back later that day. He called back to the missus,

'You go on to the hotel, love, I'll have a couple of drinks with the lads and I'll join you later.'

He never did. It got to about seven-ish and he was still with us. We said,

'When are you supposed to be flying back?'

Andy looked at his watch and said, 'About now.'

It didn't seem to bother him and, knowing Andy, he had probably planned it! He asked if we had anywhere to bunk down. He had no clothes other than what he was in. He stayed with us, taking most of Mike Milligan's clothes. Mike went mad. Andy kipped in our room, mine and Ronnie's because I was out a lot. After a couple of days the Scottish press were beginning to gather outside our hotel. Rangers had paid for his flight and were getting anxious about his welfare. They sent someone out to bring him home.

On another trip, Mike Lyons came down the road. He had a tie round his head, a ripped t-shirt, shorts and flip-flops. He also had a bottle of schnapps in his hand. He sat down and ordered another bottle of schnapps straight away. Soon we were doing schnapps in one, along with the beer. We started a drinking game where we all had to change clothes, the idea being that you had to swap an item with the person next to you . . . Mike ended up with a new set of clothes on, quite decent. Eventually he left and arranged to meet us again, either that evening or the next day. I can't remember! We swerved that one! He was difficult to keep up with. Phil Black, a mate of mine who had gone over with me on the trip, complained,

'I've just given him an £80 shirt in exchange for a ripped t-shirt!'

We limited the drinking games on holiday because you could get hammered far too quickly and that wasn't the object. It was a marathon, not a sprint. The aim was to be the last man standing.

There were plenty of great lads 'on tour'. Nick Henry, Mike Milligan and Ian Marshall were all good value. My mate Ronnie Evans actually got a job at Oldham Athletic because he ate a drinks bill in Magaluf! Ronnie used to play for City but had injured his ankle. It was an end of season trip to the sun and we took Ronnie with us. We were all sitting in the bar one day and asked for the bill. When it came Ronnie asked for some tomato sauce. The waitress brought it, Ronnie put a dollop on the bill and promptly ate it! When the waitress came back for the money, Ronnie said to her,

'What bill?'

Joe was sitting on the terrace outside and called me over.

'We need to find Ronnie a job, SOSS. We need a kit man and he can help you as well.' Joe had recognised something in Ronnie that would fit in well with the Oldham ethos. He saw him as someone who could reduce tension and the day-to-day strain. There is monotony and intensity around football clubs and you need a certain type of characters to do that. Typical of this approach was the time when Joe brought in local DJ Mike Sweeney to training. Sweeney's enthusiasm was unbelievable. Result? The mood in the camp was immediately lifted.

Nick Henry was never far from the action such as in an end of season trip to Corfu when a group of us got into a misunderstanding in a pavement cafe bar. I think I was the only member of staff who went that year although a couple of directors were in charge of the party. Things had been quiet until then. There hadn't been much to do on the trip as we'd been booked into a remote part of the island.

Next door to the bar was a shop with racks of stuff on display outside. Nick got some after sun cream off one of the racks, squirted it in his hand, put it on and returned the bottle to the shelf. Unsurprisingly, the shop owner wasn't best pleased and insisted that Nick paid for the whole bottle. Nick said he would pay for the squirt but the shop keeper didn't share his sense of humour. Before we knew what was happening a number of scooters turned up. There must have been seven at least. In the meantime, the culprit and others had scarpered, leaving just Frank Bunn and me stranded there with a bunch of locals in front of us hellbent on getting their own back for their mate, the shop keeper. It was too late to run and it started to get a bit ugly. I suppose we could have paid but because they had sent for these people to come and rough us up my brain went in the opposite direction and I resisted. They fancied their chances with me because when it came to size and physicality there was just no comparison between me and Frank. Now Frankie Bunn is an absolute gem of a man. He was a tough, uncompromising striker who never squirmed out of challenges. As a person he was very loyal and, boy, did I need him at that moment! All I can remember is Frank picking people off my back and slinging them across the pavement. He stood and helped me in my hour of need and we survived. I didn't condone what Nick did in the first place but you can't always control what lads get up to.

A group of us were all sitting round on the pavement at a cafe/bar in Magaluf one morning. This was in the Oldham days once again. One or two of the lads were feeling worse for wear whilst others had been in the sun a bit too long the previous day and were burning up.

A van pulled up, a bloke got out, slid up the door at the back and removed a box which he took into one of the shops. My mate Phil Black was with us again and about to do something he was to regret. You won't find Phil's name in the annals of Oldham players. He had a shop in Manchester. It was one of the original boutique-type menswear shops. A lot of United and City players visited and Phil got friendly with them as well as becoming mates with Ron Atkinson, who was, of course, big friends with Joe Royle. This is how Blackie arrived on the scene. He started coming to games with us, usually travelling independently. It got to the point where he and another lad, John Peers, started sitting on the bench at home games. John was a hairdresser and many of the players were customers. Ron went to see him as well. Eventually, they both got into Ron's games at the Cliff. The two of them used to sit on the bench with us at quite a few games. One of the directors asked a question for Joe at a board meeting,

'Mr. Royle, who are those two gentlemen who sit on the bench with you?'

'They are my friends. Why, is there a problem?'

And it wasn't mentioned again!

Anyway, Blackie was a funny guy and back in Magaluf he decided to play a prank. As the van drove off he noticed the back left open and instinctively pulled a box out. It was full of sun cream. He took some bottles out and decided they would be useful. I told him to put them back and leave the box on the pavement. The van driver would realise that the box was missing and come back for it. It sounded like a simple solution.

A few minutes later the driver returned with the police. Blackie was nicked and frogmarched away to the police station. I asked the policeman how long they would be with him and he suggested that our friend wouldn't be long.

We carried on drinking and a couple of hours went by. There was still no sign of Blackie. More time passed and I decided to go up to the police station with John Hallsworth. As we approached, Blackie was outside and when he saw us coming towards him he started shaking his hand to motion us away.

I ignored him, and marched straight in to the police station. Two hours had now been about four and this just wasn't good enough. I protested and both John and I finished up in the cells! John's saying; 'You can't do this. I came up here of my own accord.' We called John 'Captain Darling' after the Blackadder character. There were likenesses between the two and John was very much the sensible sort.

Apparently, the van driver had said that Blackie had stolen his radio. He had gone round the corner and taken his radio out, accusing Blackie of pinching it. I didn't know that Blackie had sorted out to pay for the sun cream but didn't have any money on him. He had been trying to tell us that he had been released and had been waiting outside for someone to take him to the hotel to get his money so that he could pay.

Over the course of the afternoon other lads followed John and myself up to the police station and each one finished up in the jail with us, about thirteen in all! In those days you had to pay a fine to get out of the cells and the more the police caged in, the more money they would take. We were convinced that they were going to put it in their back pockets. Half the lads were adamant they weren't going to pay, the other half wanted to get out as soon as possible. In the end, Blackie got back to the hotel and stumped up for all of us.

There was a lot of piss-taking on holiday. John Hallworth copped for a lot in the summer of 1990. After the Littlewoods final and FA Cup semi-final the club rewarded the players by taking them to Clearwater Beach in America for ten days. It was a bit more civilised than Magaluf but there was still plenty going on including lots of hotels with live music. We used to sit in and around the pool during the day. It was Budweiser in plastic cups. John was a strawberry blonde who didn't like to be in the sun a lot so divided his time between sun, shade and pool. Rick Holden used to say that after a while in the sun he looked like a match! John would put his plastic cup next to the pool and kept swimming back across to drink some. While he was at the other side of the pool the lads would keep filling his plastic cup with pool water! After a while, John looked up from the water and said:

'It's not so strong this Budweiser is it?' We were pissing ourselves. Then he found out and started chasing the lads who scattered in all directions.

We took one of the fans to Clearwater, local businessman Brian Ellidge. We were wandering around the hotels before coming back to ours where there was always a disco. Brian sat on one of these high bar stools. He suddenly jumped off one to have a dance and fell flat on the floor, tearing his Achilles tendon. Brian had had a few and was insistent he was ok. The alcohol must have acted as an anaesthetic! We just about managed to get him back to his room then took him to hospital next day before sending him home in a cast.

Stan Ternent favoured Vilamoura as a destination because of the many opportunities for golf in the Portuguese sun. On one occasion, Micky Mellon had gone out drinking and went missing for a couple of days. He arrived back on the morning of the third day, still in the same gear. I was having a swim in the pool and all you could hear coming out of the apartment that he shared with Ian Wright and Mitchell Thomas was

Micky's screaming and shouting. The other two had obviously stripped him off for a shower. I was doing my breast stroke across the pool when suddenly, 'Splash!' a trainer landed in the water next to me, followed a short while later by another . . . . I don't remember Micky ever booking a holiday himself. There was a girl called Angela at Burnley. If you wanted anything Ange would do it. She'd say, 'Where do you want to go to?' and the rest would be sorted.

One year we were taken to the Seychelles. It was a bit different from the usual haunts, out in the Indian Ocean, and the visit included a match against the Seychelles team. I don't think most of the lads had a clue as to where it was really. The 1992-93 season had just finished. It was our second season back in the top flight but the first of the new Premier League.

We had started well and were in mid-table after a dozen games or so. This was followed by a dismal run which left us bottom with ten games to play. Basically, we looked dead and buried with three games left. Not only did we have to win all three but hope that Crystal Palace gained no more than one point from their last two games. We played Aston Villa away in a televised Sky game. Villa were second and needed a win themselves to have any hope of winning the title. Nick Henry scored the only goal midway through the first half to give us hope of staying up and hand the title to Manchester United. Three days later, we beat Liverpool at Boundary Park while Palace drew at Manchester City. To survive we had to beat fellow-strugglers Southampton at home on the last day and hope that Palace lost at Arsenal.

It was an unbelievable game for us. At 4-1 we were cruising but I'll never forget a fifteen-minute period when Matt Le Tissier single-handedly took the game by the scruff of the neck and hauled his side back into the game. He was virtually unplayable and to add to the drama we were hearing that Palace were behind at Arsenal. For the final few minutes, the fans were on the touchline willing us on and creeping on to the playing surface. We won 4-3 and stayed up. You can imagine our joy as everyone had expected us to be relegated.

Celebrations followed then we all had to report at the ground the next morning, Seychelles bound. The trip had already been set-up and it was a good job we hadn't been relegated. As it was, the lads were buzzing. We headed for Heathrow by bus and started to tackle crates of Budweiser. Supplies had run out by the time we got to the Midlands so we had to stop for more. We checked in at the airport but the flight was delayed so there was an overnight stay in London. This was a further opportunity to get bladdered. By the time we boarded I was a right mess and so were many of the others. Plenty of brown bags were provided just in case. I had a bit of a kip and came round.

We were supposed to play the game on the Monday but because of the delay it was postponed until the following Saturday which meant that we had the whole week there. We were given a hotel in a remote part of the island because the hotel we were supposed to be in, in a busier part, was being renovated. The one we were given turned out to be a hotel for romantic, newly-married couples. Joe's orders were clear,

'I don't mind what you do during the week but Friday is an eleven 'o' clock curfew before the game.'

We started having a good piss up. We found a casino on the opposite side of the island, near where we should have been. We had been advised not to leave the hotel and wander as the surrounding forests were full of wild animals and there were prostitutes and pimps all over the place. They would zoom in, especially in the casino. They offered rides home but we reckoned that if we accepted we wouldn't be seen again. Our answer was to take taxis each way but they cost us a fortune, maybe £100 a trip. When we got back we dived into the pool. There was water polo and a volleyball net. We played both into the early hours. The lights would eventually start to go on in the hotel rooms, people would come on to balconies and shout to us to keep the noise down.

Part of the time was to be spent coaching in the villages. We made two visits. Having driven across to one village by minibus all we found were empty mud huts with a bare, barren area in the middle. The only grass was in tufts. Undeterred, we got out and started to set up the cones and balls. With no one there it was an eerie place. We stood in the middle and marked out our area. Gradually, villagers started to come cautiously from the shadows. Eventually, there must have been hundreds of them and all the kids were barefoot. When we noticed that, all our plans went out of the window. However, we managed and it was a real eye-opener.

On Friday, curfew night, Mike Milligan decided not to obey the rule set by Joe. There was a night club in the hotel. We were the only ones in it and Mike just wouldn't stop drinking. Joe stepped in and what followed was like a scene from the Keystone Cops. Joe had a go at Milly who replied, something on the lines of,

'Fuck off fathead'.

Over the next half hour or so Joe chased Milly round the hotel! We sat in reception and watched the entertainment unfold. The lift door kept opening and Milly would come out.

'Where's he gone?'

'That way,' we pointed.

So Milly would go the opposite way. Joe would emerge,

'Where's he gone?'

'That way'.

Milly eventually gave up and went to bed.

The game kicked off at three 'o' clock and it was the hottest part of the day. Joe picked his first eleven and included Mike Milligan.

'The best way of dealing with this,' said Joe, 'is to go three up as soon as you can, otherwise it will get hard as they are more used to the conditions. Take the sting out of them then you can ease off and pass it around'.

We kicked off and rolled the ball back to Milly who promptly fell over it. Joe said to me,

'Little sod, he's playing the full 90 minutes.'

We went three nil up, as planned and there were mass changes at half time, even I went on. Willie Donachie was another substitute. There would be no relaxing out there on Willie's watch. Joe went round everyone apart from Milly, who was just keeping quiet. We had put cold towels on him and steam was coming through. Back out he went for the second forty-five. Milly was breathing through his arse by the end and spluttering even more than normal. It was Joe's way of telling his player that what he had done was unacceptable.

Before we had left England, Joe said to me,

'We have one spare place left. Choose one of the young lads and he will be at the beck and call of you and the players for all the time we are out there.'

I chose Neil Tolson and we had him on a piece of string. Every time he sat down we timed it for him to get up again to answer another request! I have to say that Tolly took it in good part. He was a gem and went on to have a decent career with a lot of goals. I next bumped into him when he was manager of Hyde. He remembered the Seychelles!

We had a lot of time to make our own entertainment during the week and arranged to go deep sea fishing one day. Graeme Sharp, Neil Pointon, Mike Milligan, Nick Henry, Ronnie Evans and myself were on board. Fortunately, we had someone to skipper the boat and all our gear was properly laid out for us. Milly was sick when he was out there but we all had a good time and I seem to remember all of us catching some fish. One of the fish was a Marlin. It's a spectacular sight with its spear-like snout and some can reach over sixteen feet in length. The skipper of the boat wanted it and, traditionally, they are handed over as part of the service provided and a chance for the local to make some money. However, we paid him on this occasion and took the fish back for the chef in the hotel to cook for us that night. It was delicious!

The week was a fantastic experience. I had a beautiful room and a cracking view across the sea. It was a fairy-tale type of location and we took what we could out of it. It wasn't Magaluf, though! Fortunately, with the results going our way at the end of the season we could celebrate in style. That's why it was so memorable.

Chapter Twenty-Five

THE SACRIFICES YOU MAKE

Inevitably, my family life suffered. I packed my bags and left three marriages.

I t's a ten month season now, a long time together and it can be a slog, particularly if things aren't going right—training, playing, training, travelling, hotels, playing . . . . You had to have a certain mindset to deal with it. You become obsessed with the game. By the time I left the north-east, in the early stages of my career, I was already well-aware of how football takes over. I had spent two years on the merry-go-round. Newcastle United was absolutely full-on. The club took over your life. The city is a long way up the country and there were some very long journeys backwards and forwards. Sunderland was the next nearest place, then Middlesbrough but beyond that it was Leeds. It got to the stage where I used to count the lamp-posts on the way back up the A1! I could tell you from certain landmarks exactly how long the rest of the journey was going to be!

Newcastle chairman, Stan Seymour, once said to me, 'You could have a job here for life'. It was possible back then. There were fewer managerial changes affecting the physiotherapists' union. I'd had a ball on Tyneside and it kick started my career. I just didn't want to stay up there for the rest of my time in the game. Joe Royle taught me that there is a lot more to life than football. Don't get me wrong, Joe was ultra-professional and a winner but he also had a knack of getting everything into perspective. He would stress that a bad result didn't compare with experiencing warfare or poverty. My move to Oldham was an effort to re-dress the balance in my professional and personal life, bring in a bit of playing again, do some clinic work and get back into my old circle of friends around Manchester and the north-west. I failed to achieve that. Unfortunately, despite trying to keep those aspects of life going, the family still took a back seat as I threw myself into my job for the team, my countless games with the lads at the Cliff and in the charity matches and my social life in and around the lads. I didn't want football to dominate my life but it did. I loved the banter and was never able to resist the magnetic force that the game exerted on me.

Inevitably, my family life suffered. I packed my bags and left three marriages. I walked out on two whilst at Boundary Park with a third to follow at Burnley. I'm not proud of the fact that I'm on my fourth marriage now but it's happened. It's hard to maintain normality in this crazy game of football. There is undeniably a buzz being around football teams, adrenalin flows, you are a long time away from home and temptations come your way. I've always had a wandering eye and have enjoyed chatting to the girls. I was quite a lad in my day. All my marriages have involved really nice girls but there was something in me that caused me to stray from the straight and narrow. Football certainly opens doors, particularly when you are at a league club. I succumbed on more than one occasion leading to ultimatums along the lines of:

'Stop what you are doing or pack your bags and go'.

My previous wives would probably say that football didn't break things up but the lifestyle that the game gave me caused issues to develop. I just loved being in the limelight and thrilled at the sort of life that football gave me. I don't think I would be on my fourth marriage now had I been in another profession or an office. A lot of physios I meet outside the game have said to me:

'Why do you bother putting yourself through all that emotional agony?'

They make a good point but the game is in my blood. Football has always been part of my life, both a pressure and a relief. I've ruined marriages but travelled the world. I've split families and lost friends along the way but had some brilliant experiences with the lads. I've missed my children growing up. I would be out as they were waking up and back around nine after they had gone to bed. The only chance to see them was at weekends and even that depended on match commitments.

You meet a lot of people in the game but it's not easy to maintain close friendships. I keep in regular touch with my best mates such as Ronnie Evans, Micky Mellon and Craig Madden but there are so many former colleagues where I will think,

'Mmm, not spoken to him for a while . . . I'll give him a ring . . . No, I'll leave it till tomorrow . . . then again, next week will do.'

Before you know it a month or even a year has passed and you've still not done anything about it. There are so many 'ships that pass in the night' in football. When you do actually meet up you don't tend to talk about the game, more likely the scrapes you got into, the fun you had:

'Do you remember that time when such and such a thing happened?'

'Aye, who was it who threw that . . . ?'

It's more about recalling the funny stories. That's the way it is with me and I suspect countless others who have had a career in football. I went to Cammel Laird's one day. It's a semi-professional club based in Birkenhead and I immediately saw three lads who I hadn't seen for thirty years. They were very welcoming and we started reminiscing straight away but the moment came and went. Suddenly, they were gone and I may not see them again.

'I'll ring you and we'll go out for a drink.' Twelve months later you still haven't.

All your focus is on doing well as a team. You want success and are part of the team that is driving towards certain goals. You suffer from tunnel-vision because of it. I devoted too much of my time entirely to football and other aspects of my life suffered because of it.

I've now come full circle in my footballing journey. I started on the edge of the game making my first steps under Bryan Hamilton at Tranmere Rovers, moved into the limelight at Newcastle and Oldham, before returning back to more modest surroundings in non-league football in my beloved Manchester area. Deep into the writing of this book yet another opportunity came my way. I'm part of the League Medical Association and have kept my membership up. I got an email from them mentioning a job at Macclesfield Town. I knew Mel Pejic, the Macclesfield physio, from Stoke City days so rang him for some background. Mel told me that he was going back to Stoke as head of their academy and asked if I was interested in the Macclesfield position. He explained what it involved and told me that he would have a word with the manager John Askey. John rang me the next day. We met up on Christmas Eve 2013 and I started a few days later after making sure everything was covered at Radcliffe.

Macclesfield Town (Pictures courtesy of www.peterhiltonphotography.co.uk)

Macclesfield's a lovely club with bags of tradition. They are a decent side who play good football which is always important to me. Soon after starting we were at home to Sheffield Wednesday in the FA Cup. The match received plenty of coverage in the media and it was a taste once again of what I had sampled so much earlier in my career. I finish training around two-ish and can still go and do my clinics in the afternoon and evening. I still work with Ronnie in the clinic at Radcliffe.

I had no intention of going back full-time but always thought that if something suitable came up in the Manchester area I'd be interested. Macclesfield tend to travel on the day so that suits me well. My days of regular overnight stops are behind me and I also do a clinic into Friday evening so that would have been affected. The move fits the bill. Hopefully it is my last chance in football and I can go out and enjoy it.

I've blazed a trial through my life and to those who I upset along the way I offer my apologies. I'm not proud of some of what I've done but those mistakes can't be undone. If I lived it all over again I wouldn't want to be married four times but I've had a wonderful time and sampled life at every level from non-league to international football. I've had the honour of working with some of the greats. I've experienced promotion and relegation and had a ball both on and off the pitch.

I've now found happiness and stability and come through a process of maturing. Dad often said, 'When are you going to grow up?' At last I think I have. Through all my escapades I've got there. Don't get me wrong. Life's still fun but I approach it all from a different angle. I've learnt to look at things from other people's points of view and to be less selfish.

Now I can finally combine my role in football with being there for my kids at events like school assemblies and concerts. I am married to Sandra, a girl who has no interest in football.

With Sandra, Ruby and Alfie

She might recognise a player if he has been on television for a different reason like Beckham. This is a blessing because it brings you back down to earth. When Sandra and I got married, Mum, bless her soul, said to me:

'Do me a favour, Ian, make this your last wedding.'

MY BEST TEAM

Based on players who I have worked with or played alongside

T here are so many 'Best of . . .' selections that just seem to concentrate on choosing the best individuals without taking into account the set-up of the team as a whole. I've looked back at the many professionals that I've had the honour to work with and produced a team which offers balance and solidity as well as the entertainment value that has always attracted me to football. There will be one or two surprises, no doubt, but football has always been a game of opinions and I've never been short of my own! My team is versatile enough to play both 4-2-4 and 4-3-3 and contains individuals who have regularly won matches through their own genius. Finally, these lads could have some cracking nights away!

Goalkeeper: **Andy Goram (Oldham Athletic)**

The best goalkeeper and shot stopper I have worked with.

Right-back: **Denis Irwin (Oldham Athletic)**

His career was resurrected by Joe Royle and Willie Donachie and taken to new heights by Sir Alex Ferguson. Good enough to play at right-back or left and the best full-back that I've worked with.

Centre-back:　　**Earl Barrett (Oldham Athletic)**

A real gentleman who could look after himself. A class act.

Centre-back:　　**Richard Jobson (Oldham Athletic)**

Never shirked a challenge. Jobbo would head a brick out of the area and then ask questions. He mixed it with some of the game's most physical attackers.

Left-back:　　**Neil Pointon (Oldham Athletic)**

A strong defender who played at the highest level. His left foot could club a ball the length of the pitch.

Midfield:　　**Terry McDermott (Newcastle United)**

The Racehorse. Played, trained and drank with never-ending energy.

Midfield:　　**Paul Gascoigne (Newcastle United/Burnley)**

The best midfield player of his generation

Forward:　　**Chris Waddle (Newcastle United)**

Lured defenders in then beat them off either foot. Offers my team flexibility. Magical in midfield for Marseille.

Forward:　　**Kevin Keegan (Newcastle United)**

Top player, top bloke. An amazing and inspirational professional.

Forward:　　**Peter Beardsley (Newcastle United)**

He loved everything about the game and was capable of doing anything with a football in front of him.

Forward: **Jamie Vardy (Fleetwood Town)**

The biggest surprise for many of you but based on the impact that he had at Fleetwood. Scored goals that won games.

<u>Substitutes:</u>

I've gone for a lot of attacking options, showing my natural instinct to make football entertaining to watch.

Forward: **Ian Wright (Burnley)**

Could look after himself and turned a match in a moment.

Forward: **Graeme Sharp (Oldham Athletic)**

Strong as an ox, great in the air, fantastic touch . . . . a proper striker.

Forward: **Andy Ritchie (Oldham Athletic)**

His first touch always put him on to his second. He never had to adjust his movement. Smooth and silky, everything done with consummate ease.

Forward: **Frank Worthington (Bolton Wanderers Vets)**

A bit of a tenuous link but I played alongside the king of the tricksters on many occasions. An unpredictably talented crowd-pleaser.

Goalkeeper: **Bruce Grobelaar (Football League XI)**

A decision based on the impact of just one game, the centenary match at Windsor Park, Belfast, in 1990. There's not much between Goram and Grobelaar so perhaps one for each half.

Defender/Midfield/Forward: **Paul Warhurst (Oldham Athletic)**

Has the versatility to give cover across the pitch.

Midfield: **Vinny Jones**

Didn't work with him as a player but a character who impressed me a lot when we met up. Adds steel to midfield and would entertain us in the bar afterwards with his stories!

32082377R00144

Printed in Great Britain
by Amazon